In Visible Light

In Visible Light

Photography and Classification in Art, Science and The Everyday

Curated by Russell Roberts

Edited by Chrissie Iles and Russell Roberts

With essays by Elizabeth Edwards, David Elliott, Russell Roberts and Abigail Solomon-Godeau

Museum of Modern Art Oxford

Acknowledgements

With thanks to the following collectors, galleries and institutions whose invaluable support has made this exhibition possible:

Autograph, the Association of Black Photographers

The Bethlem Royal Hospital, London

Bibliothèque Interuniversitaire de Médecine, Paris

Birmingham City Library

Karl Blossfeldt Archive, Ann and Jürgen Wilde, Cologne

Bolton Museum and Art Gallery

The British Museum, Department of Ethnography, Museum of Mankind

Terry Dennett Jo Spence Archive

Paula Cooper Gallery, New York

Helga de Alvear Gallery, Madrid

The English Heritage

Fonds Régional d'Art Contemporain des Pays de la Loire

Galerie Ulrich Fiedler, Cologne

Fraenkel Gallery, San Francisco

Marian Goodman Gallery, New York and Paris

The Kinsey Institute for Research in Sex, Gender & Reproduction, Indiana University

Yvon Lambert Gallery, Paris

Audrey Linkman

Robert Miller Gallery, New York

Musée des Collections Historiques de la Préfecture de Police, Paris

National Museum of Photography, Film & Television, Bradford

New York City Department of Public Records

Maureen Paley, Interim Art

The Pitt Rivers Museum, University of Oxford, School of Anthropology and Museum Ethnography

Royal Anthropological Institute of Great Britain and Ireland

Torch Gallery, Amsterdam

The Royal Photographic Society, Bath

The Royal Society of Medicine, London

August Sander Archiv/SK Stiftung Kultur, Cologne

Saatchi Collection, London

Sonnabend Gallery, New York

The Library, University College London

The Wiener Library, London

Michael and Jane Wilson Collection

And thanks to those lenders who wish to remain anonymous.

Contents

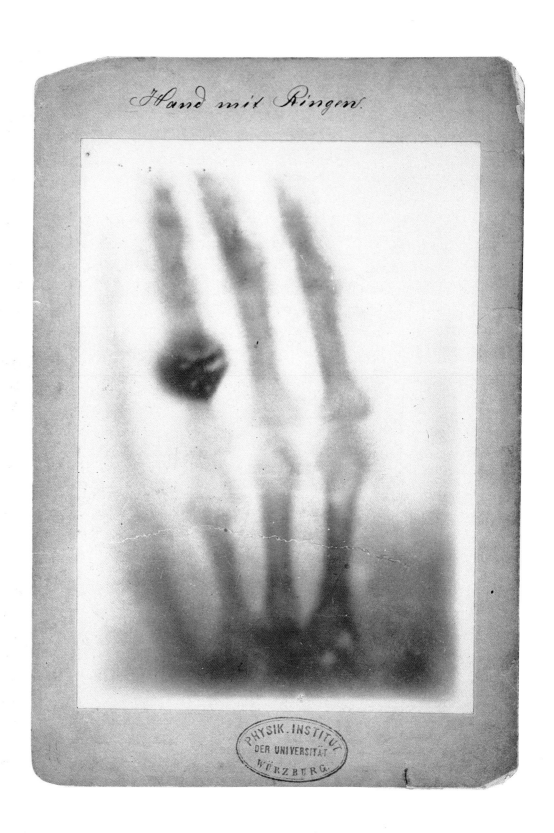

Wilhelm von Roentgen

The bones of a hand with a ring on one finger, viewed through X-ray

1895

Foreword

It has been a pleasure to begin as Director of the Museum of Modern Art Oxford during *In Visible Light: Photography and Classification in Art, Science and The Everyday.* The concept of this important exhibition, begun under the guidance of former Director David Elliott, coincides with the direction that we would now like to take the Museum programme. Crossing over conventional boundaries of time, space and nationality, as well as blurring the line between science and art, *In Visible Light* points to a new way of understanding visual culture by ironically breaking down modernism's tendency toward classification and segregation. A complex and innovative exhibition, *In Visible Light* has involved the dedicated efforts of many individuals. We are especially grateful to its curator, Russell Roberts, for his provocative curatorial approach in revealing the numerous contradictory histories and meanings underpinning the ways in which we have attempted to order the world through the photographic image, from the nineteenth century to the present.

The exhibition has been made possible through the generous sponsorship of Oxford University Press. We are also most grateful to the Elephant Trust for their support of this catalogue. We would also like to acknowledge the generous support of the Cooper Charitable Trust, The Embassy of the United States of America and the Canadian High Commission.

In the realisation of this project, both Russell Roberts and the curatorial staff at MoMA are most grateful for the support and advice of Ron Cowdery, Judith Clark, John Dutton, Elizabeth Edwards, David Elliott, Colin Harding, Mark Haworth-Booth, Pete James, David Jones, Professor Anne Massey and the Media Arts Faculty of the Southampton Institute, Aileen McLaughlin, Lydia Papadamitrio, Jennifer Pearson-Yamashiro, Chris Phipps, Pam Roberts, Helen Simpson, Abigail Solomon-Godeau, Chris Titterington, Michael and Jane Wilson and Fred Vermorel. Russell Roberts would particularly like to thank Alia Al-Khalidi, Mark Durden, Stephen Foster, Hilary Roberts and Godfrey Worsdale for their comments and support during the research and planning of the exhibition. The project could not have come to fruition without the indefatigable commitment and hard work of its co-ordinator at MoMA, Astrid Bowron. We are also grateful to Chrissie Iles, Head of Exhibitions, for her important contribution to the project. Elena Fernandez and Clare Manchester provided valuable assistance, and the installation crew worked with tremendous effort and care in order to realise the complex installation of the exhibition. We are grateful to the Museum's Council of Management for their continued support of this project. Finally, we would like to extend our deep gratitude to all the artists, institutions and private lenders, and to all the curators and archivists whose valuable assistance has made this exhibition possible.

Kerry Brougher
Director

Thomas Struth

National Gallery I, London

1989

Taxonomy

Some Notes Towards the Histories of Photography and Classification

Russell Roberts

In 1870, the Berlin Society for Anthropology commissioned Carl W. Dammann, a commercial photographer based in Hamburg, to produce a body of photographs that reflected the anthropological and ethnographic differences of various races. This project aimed to continue methods of documentation which accorded with a widening anthropological interest in the photograph as evidence. The way in which this evidence was configured is significant, as it marks the intersection of various genres of, and conflicting investments in, photography which were present in its different scientific uses between 1850 and 1900. In this context, the overlapping uses of photography as document contain contradictions that undermine the stability of classifications established in the natural and human sciences during the nineteenth century.

Dammann's album, *Anthropologisch — Ethnologisches Album in Photographien* (1873–76) is typological, moving from physical anthropology to ethnography in order to describe differences and similarities between various indigenous groups of Europe, Asia, America and Africa. The album testifies not only to the range of identities and cultures on display but, more openly, to the practice of photography as it moved between the expanding visual cultures of commerce and science. For example, Dammann combined approved material for anthropological study with re-photographed cartes-de-visite and cabinet prints, whose original currency was rooted in popular consumption of the "exotic" rather than in scientifically-produced evidence of ethnic types.

The Dammann album evokes a number of projects in the nineteenth century in which photographers, intellectually removed from the discourses to which they were contributing, were commissioned to make photographs as evidence for theories that organised knowledge around the body, disease and culture.[1] Pictorial codes and conventions from other disciplines and genres permeated the photograph as document as it moved through various discourses. The tensions between photographic conventions and scientific method begin to fray the edges of both the taxonomic arrangement of the subject and the rigid archival ordering of images.

The significance of Dammann in relation to this exhibition lies primarily with the inconsistencies of the album as a particular kind of scientific document.[2] Dammann's use of commercial material provides a conspicuous route into undermining some of the premises of classification and archival uses of photography which early scientific institutions uses sought to establish. In this *collection* of images we encounter the objectification and spectacle of "other" cultures, the intersection of the various gazes that passed over the bodies of those photographed, and which were then homogenised by typological display and the act of photographing that conceals other realities. Dammann's sleight of hand reveals the reductive and limited nature of traditional archival models of knowledge that used the "type" as an organising principle.

This introduction outlines certain elements that led to the questioning of the archival or taxonomic paradigm which came to govern many uses of photography and, by extension, culture and society. *In Visible Light* draws attention to the overlapping of photographic practices and taxonomic methods, from documentary evidence to a formalist aesthetic and ideological critique. The relationships between pornography, commercial portraiture, art practice and scientific research can be traced through many of the photographs presented here. For example, Henry Hering's portraits of patients at Bethlem Royal Hospital are entwined with the codes of respectability found in commercial portraiture. Baron Wilhelm von Gloeden's use of arcadian themes and ethnological values are deployed to offset the homo-erotic content of his studies of young Sicilian males. The overt reference to strip-tease in Eadweard Muybridge's sequential images of a young woman photographed during *Miscellaneous Phases of the Toilet* (1887) sits ambiguously between passive physiological document and an eroticising gaze. The classical physiognomies derived from museum artefacts in Francis Galton's composites, the references to art history in the typology of insanity by Dr. Hugh Diamond and the representations of hysteria at Salpêtrière, Paris, intersect with the photographic document in different ways. This network of references reveals the mediations and influences caught in the flow of visual culture, paralleling the development of modernity itself.[3]

Allan Sekula's essay *The Body and the Archive* describes the continuation of an archival method in photography that is present in the modernist poetics of Walker Evans and, ideologically, in the computer-generated composites of Nancy Burson. The essay explores Positivism's investment in the photograph as truth, and how this, combined with an archival approach, came to define and regulate the criminal body. The archive is discussed here as a space in which the control of deviance could take place, and the archival arrangement moves between the typological and the individual in Sekula's analysis of the visual methods of the eugenicist Francis Galton (1883), and the police photographer Alphonse Bertillon (1893). Sekula's contextual study of these two very different practices takes up most of the essay, and it is the reference to an extended archival paradigm which suggests other perspectives from which to unpack classification in the contexts of modernism and postmodernism.[4]

In Visible Light draws attention to a paradox which has surrounded the status of the photograph from early accounts of the medium involving the dual role of the photograph as either art or science. The exhibition explores the exchanges between these roles in the context of classification. The influence of an archival mode of photography is evident in the formalism of the documentary work of, for example, Eugene Atget, Walker Evans, Karl Blossfeldt and August Sander, and in fine art photography from the 1960s onwards. The inclusion of work by artists such as Bernd and Hilla Becher and Ed Ruscha is not simply an illustration of methodological or stylistic lineage. Douglas Crimp described how finding Ruscha's bookwork *Twentysix Gasoline Stations* (1963) in the section on transportation in the New York Public Library, demonstrated how its presumed function caused it to be mis-catalogued. "The fact that there is nowhere for *Twentysix Gasoline Stations* within the present system of classification is an index of the book's radicalism with respect to established modes of thought."[5] This example of taxonomic resistance relies on the mutability of the photograph. As an aesthetic device, the formal connection to classificatory modes is also open to question, as it is seen in relation to earlier taxonomic uses of photography, and the issues this raises in the context of science.

The bringing together of new and old taxonomies forces a comparison between different historical periods which creates its own classificatory logic. Museums have been integral to devising and implementing classificatory schemes. Their presence is, paradoxically, both in the foreground and the shadow of *In Visible Light*. Stephen Greenblatt described two models for the presentation of artworks in museums in his essay *Resonance and Wonder*, which present possibilities for exploring categories through display:

> One [is] centred on what I shall call resonance and the other on wonder. By *resonance* I mean the power of the displayed object to reach out beyond its formal boundaries to a larger world, to evoke in the viewer the complex, dynamic cultural forces from which it has emerged and for which it may be taken by the viewer to stand. By *wonder* I mean the power of the displayed object to stop the viewer in his or her tracks, to convey an arresting sense of uniqueness, to evoke an exalted attention.[6]

These two models of visual experience are often intertwined. Through strategic juxtapositions, the exhibition adopts an approach which has sympathies with Greenblatt's definition of "resonance". Some of the combinations within the exhibition invite a reassessment of the reductive nature of classification and the perceived literal power of images.

Roger Fenton
Greek Hero c. 1857
Sculpture of
Hermaphrodite c. 1855
Study of Bust of
Woman c. 1850

The invention of photography in the late 1830s paralleled the rise of the modern museum in Europe. The museum's ordering principles were often hierarchical or evolutionary, and used narratives of progress to define a shift from nature to culture, or from primitive to civilised societies. Roger Fenton's detailed photographs of objects in the British Museum (*c. 1855*) were part of a commission to compile a visual inventory of its collections, and to make these records commercially available. The photographs functioned originally as documents, but as Fenton moved between genres of photography, his work is often homogenised under the rubric of art. In *Axis: A tale of two stories* (1995) Vid Ingelevics responds to the reinvention of Fenton's museum work as art in certain histories of photography by diagrammatically separating its different representations, revealing how Fenton's photographs were spatially organised to function as art in the museum and document in the library.

The question of originality in relation to the capacity of photography for infinite reproduction is explored in the work of Sherrie Levine. Levine's approach addresses a specific history of photography's

Vid Ingelevics
*Axis: a tale of two
stories*
1995

role within museum and modernist discourse, in terms of authorship, authenticity and presence. Levine's appropriation of a photograph by Walker Evans in *Untitled (After Walker Evans: Negative)* (1989) undermines the museum's value system, where emphasis is placed on the original rather than the copy, drawing attention to the photographic process itself.

Karen Knorr's *The Invention of Tradition* (1988) and *The Physiognomy of Taste* (1990) approach the museum in terms of the ideology of its rules and etiquette in the construction of taste. Knorr's images show how collections embody an expression of power through ownership and display. Using irony, she contests the hegemony of the museum, connoisseurship and the accumulation of cultural capital. Richard Ross engages in a similar questioning by revealing the mundane characteristics of museums' visible and concealed spaces. Rooms dedicated to, for example, taxidermy and conservation evoke a sense of entropy and disorder, as do Ross's images of decayed exhibits, which counter the perception of the museum as a timeless vacuum.

Joan Fontcuberta

Fauna: Cercopithecus Icarocornu

Archive of Professor Peter Ameisenhaufen, c. 1940

1987

Sherrie Levine
Untitled (After Walker Evans: Negative)
1989

Richard Ross

Deyrolle Taxidermy, Paris, France

1985

Karen Knorr
The Physiognomy of Taste
1990

Hiroshi Sugimoto
*The Brides in the
Bath Murderer*
1994

In Joan Fontcuberta's work *Fauna* (1987–90), the rhetoric of the photograph as scientific evidence and the techniques of display combine to produce a plausible fiction. The contingency of the fantastic beasts presented here is offset through the detailed labelling of artefacts, notebooks, laboratory observations, field photographs and ephemera from the fictitious archives of Professor Ameisenhaufen. Taxonomic systems and photography conspire to produce a credible history of Ameisenhaufen's research. Fontcuberta touches on the subjectivity of knowledge and how "truth" is constructed through photography and its accompanying scientific methods of classification.

Rosamond Wolff Purcell shares a similar fascination with the bizarre and the unfamiliar in her exploration of museum language. Purcell photographs objects found in proto-museum forms such as the cabinet of curiosities, popular during the sixteenth century. In one series, she photographs objects in the collection of Peter the Great, which were used both to edify and entertain. *Arm Holding Eye Socket, Collection Albinus, Leiden* (1992) shows an anatomical preparation by the Dutch embalmer Frederik Ruysch, in which an allegorical theme is suggested by the suspending of an eye-socket from the fingers of the hand. The objects in Purcell's photographs refer to an order of things that was erased and dismissed by "rational" classifications determined by Enlightenment thought.

The allure of the grotesque in the work of Purcell is also present in Hiroshi Sugimoto's *Wax Museums* (1994), a series of photographs depicting reconstructions of famous murders in wax museum tableaux. This conflation of the museal gaze with the mediation of contemporary photography echoes the current commodification of death by the media, and the morbid fascination which permeates popular consciousness in museums where murder is presented as entertainment.

Rosamond
Purcell
*Arm Holding
Socket, Coll
Albinus, Lei*
1992

Sir Benjamin
Stone Collection
An Electric Spark,
Positive discharge
photo by M.A.A.
Campbell Swinton
1902

Sir Benjamin
Stone Collection
Remains of
sculptured groups
surmounting the
tomb of Mausolos,
Greek Collection,
British Museum
1907

The collection has become a space in which an institution or individual can make claims to their own relationship to the world and its objects. The albums of the nineteenth century industrialist, traveller, photographer and politician Sir Benjamin Stone evoke Andre Malraux's idea of a "museum without walls".[7] Stone's photography and collecting incorporates the rationalities of museum systems, yet disturbs them through idiosyncratic display. The albums outline narratives of Stone's life, world view and social status, transforming objects into the miniature and the souvenir. The souvenir, as Susan Stewart observed,

> … reduces the public, the monumental, and the three dimensional into the miniature, that which can be envelopped by the body, or into two dimensional representation, that which can be appropriated within the privatised view of the individual subject. The photograph as souvenir is a logical extension of the pressed flower, the preservation of an instant in time through a reduction of physical dimensions and a corresponding increase in significance supplied by means of narrative.[8]

The macro and the micro, the visible and the invisible, the rare and the commonplace are drawn together through Stone's collecting and re-photography which, ironically, includes early examples of calotypes by William Henry Fox Talbot. For Stone, like Malraux, "photography not only secures the admittance of various objects, fragments of objects, details of objects to the museum; it is also the organising device: it reduces the now even vaster heterogeneity to a single perfect similitude".[9]

The subtle relationship between subjective aesthetic and objective document can be seen in the psychiatric work of Dr. Hugh Diamond and the commercial photographer Henry Hering. Diamond, who was Superintendent at the Surrey County Asylum in the 1850s, used photography as a means of recording the ephemeral expressions of mental illness. In a paper delivered to the Royal Society in 1856, titled *On the Application of Photography to the Physiognomic and Mental Phenomena of Insanity*, Diamond described his approach to distilling the visual elements of disease as they appeared in the expressions of his patients:

> An Asylum on a large scale supplies instances of delirium with raving fury and spitefulness, or delirium accompanied with an appearance of gaiety and pleasure in some cases, and with constant dejection and despondency in others, or imbecility of all the faculties with a stupid look of general weakness, and the Photographer catches in a moment the permanent cloud, or the passing storm or sunshine of the soul and thus enables the Metaphysician to witness and trace out the visible and invisible in one important branch of his researches into the Philosophy of the

Dr. Hugh
W. Diamond
*Portraits of the
Insane*
(plates 1 and 2)
1856

human mind … The Photographer needs, in many cases, no aid from any language of his own, but prefers to listen, with the picture before him, to the silent but telling language of nature.[10]

Diamond's poetics extend into the photographic portraits of the predominantly female patients under his supervision. As Showalter observed, "Literary and aesthetic models of femininity influenced Diamond's choice of subjects and affected the way he asked them to pose. Women were given props that symbolised, often with pathetic futility, the asylum superintendent's hope of making them conform to Victorian ideals of feminine decorum".[11] These portraits were deeply embedded in the pseudo-science of physiognomy, and represent the first attempt photographically to construct a typology of mental illness. By contrast Henry Hering, a commercial photographer, was employed by the Bethlem Royal Hospital during the 1860s to make photographic records of patients' mental states before and after treatment. Both Diamond and Hering incorporated the

Henry Hering
Acute Mania
c. 1858

Henry Hering
Acute Melancholia, Father and Son
c. 1858

conventions of popular portraiture into their photographs as a way of visually re-introducing the mentally ill to society as subjects who had passed from their pathological state into a more stable and respectable position within a Victorian understanding of "normality".

In these photographs, it is evident that on the journey from insanity to sanity, great attention was paid to details of appearance and the presentation of the self within an already existing image repertoire. "Dress is women's weakness, and in the treatment of lunacy it should be an instrument of control, and therefore of recovery".[12] The power exercised over the patient is clear in the manipulation of the subject and in the use of established pictorial codes to enforce a gender and cultural stereotype. The blunt, frontal format used to characterise the criminal, the insane and the working classes, gives way here to an appropriation of higher cultural codes of portraiture, to indicate a dignified return to sanity. As John Tagg noted, such portraits reflected the "point

D.M. Bourneville & P. Regnard

L'Iconographie Photographique de la Salpêtrière Service de M. Charcot

Plate XXVIII

1876

Jo Spence and Dr. Tim Sheard

Narratives of Dis-ease

1989

25

Alphonse Bertillon

Affaire de Colombes. Assassinat des époux Mathieu

Vue de la salle à manger

c.1900

where discourses of psychiatry, physiognomy, photographic science and aesthetics coincided and overlapped".[13]

Questions of power arise concerning the way that the female body was centralised and stereotyped in the study of "madness". Recent work by artists such as Jo Spence and Nicole Jolicoeur re-write the objectifying and disempowering gaze of medicine. For Jolicoeur, this involves the use of photographs and drawings which formed part of the studies of hysteria at Salpêtrière under the French neurologist Jean-Martin Charcot (c. 1880). Jolicoeur re-frames Charcot's influence on the representations and definitions of hysteria by editing its visual culture. *Aura Hysterica* (1992) uses original photographs of the maid Augustine, a regular "performer" in Charcot's Tuesday Lectures, whose servitude is highlighted by the fact that the details of signs of her vocation – the cap and apron – have been erased. Overlapping these images are various graphic combinations derived from drawings by Paul Richer, Charcot's colleague, to describe how sexuality figured in what became a gendered mental condition. This use of historical material by a contemporary artist underlines both the subjectivity in the making of visual records, and the references to art history so prevalent in the researches of Charcot, evident in the publication of the *Iconographie Photographique de la Salpêtrière* (1876) and the *Nouvelle Iconographie de la Salpêtrière* (1888).

Jo Spence, in collaboration with Dr. Tim Sheard, produced *Narratives of Dis-ease* (1989), a sequence of unsettling and confrontational images which mark the artist's passage through hospital treatment for breast cancer. Spence used photography to help articulate the complex range of emotions triggered by her experience. The work is, in part, a response to modern medicine's cold processing of individuals as biological specimens, and the resulting sense of "otherness". Both Spence and Jolicoeur resist the classification imposed on women by the patriarchal value system of the institutions of medicine.

The category *Crime and Degeneration* includes work undertaken by the eugenicist Francis Galton and the police photographer Alphonse Bertillon in the 1880s and 1890s. Galton's biological determinism sought out typical facial characteristics in order to isolate the criminal. In his composite portraiture, the weight of physiognomy, linked with social Darwinism, framed the criminal body. Despite the apparitional appearance of Galton's degenerate physiognomies (which were effectively erased by the composite method), Galton's claims for the photograph as evidence of his eugenic theories were still grounded, albeit rather ambiguously, in the optical empiricism of Positivist thinking.

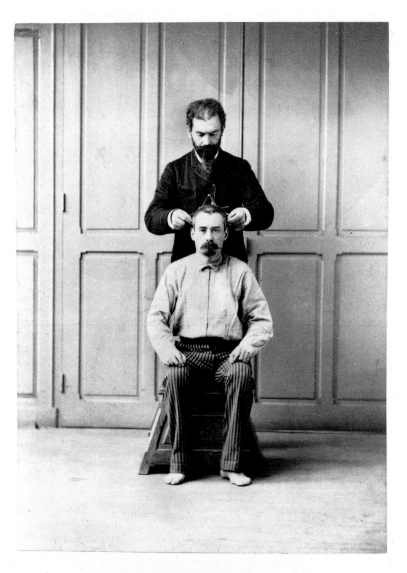

Alphonse Bertillon

Anthropometrie: mesuration du crane laterale

c.1900

Alphonse Bertillon

Assassinat de Mme Gilles. 28, rue Saint-Louis à Villemomble

Première photographie: vue du corridor, 11 octobre 1904

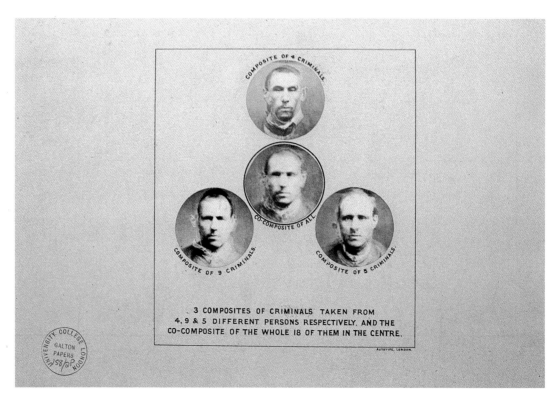

Christian Boltanski's artist's book *Archive* (1989) groups the anonymous faces of criminals and victims together in unlabelled photographs. Culled from the illustrations that fill popular crime magazines, the determinism of Galton and the physiognomic drive of his interpretation are redundant in this rather open-ended classification. For Boltanski, the anonymous portraits of victims and murderers are entwined with the sentimentality and nostalgia associated with another genre of photography – the snapshot. Andy Warhol's similar appropriation of media imagery in his series *America's Most Wanted Men* (1964) marks a fascination with the criminal as anti-hero. The bluntness of the recording and the pronounced grain of the image which they share with Boltanski's images becomes part of the criminal's visual stylistic make-up.

A selection of forensic photographs from the archives of the New York Police Department, taken around 1915, record murder scenes in which the body of the victim is still fresh from the attack. As in Bertillon's photographs, we are shown the body in its domestic context, surrounded by articles of clothing, pictures and memorabilia, from which we are able to glean something of the occupant's life, or possibly scraps of evidence, such as footprints in the snow, which offer clues to the crime.

Anon
*Scenes of crime, New York, from the New
York City Department of Records and
Information Services Municipal Archives*
c.1915

Faisal Abdu' Allah

I wanna kill uncle Sam coz he aint my mother fuckin uncle

1994

The lighting in these images, their implied narratives and the way we are invited to hover above the body of the victim suggest an intersection of these forensic studies with cinematic genres such as film noir.

The Wiener Library in London contains the archives of the Jewish Central Information Office in Amsterdam, established by Dr. Alfred Weiner in 1933 following his exile from Germany, where he had campaigned for Jewish civil rights. The J.C.I.O. collected all forms of Nazi propaganda material and general information on Nazi activities and the persecution of the Jews. In the selection of material from the Wiener Library archive in the *Crime and Degeneracy* section of the exhibition, the publication *Germany* (c. 1938) uses photography to construct myths of Aryan "purity" by evoking Nordic legends of German heritage, framed by themes drawn from Romanticism. Photographs from the newspaper *Illustrierter Beobachter* (1939) illustrate news items which pathologise the perceived "degenerate" "other" – the Jew, the gypsy and the mentally and physically unfit. The Nazi use of eugenics to remove social and ethnic "impurities", which reached its most horrific proportions during the Holocaust, demonstrates the extreme conclusion of Galton's initial Utilitarian objectives in the study of the hereditary mechanism. In stark contrast, August Sander's atlas of social types made in the Weimar Republic during the 1920s recorded the wide range of ethnic identities, social groups, professions and classes in Germany, and included portraits of individuals and groups which threatened the social and moral order. Sander, like the French photographer Eugene Atget, has tended to be subsumed within an archival model interested more in aesthetic value than in documentary content. By contrast, positioning Sander's album in relation to German Fascist propaganda from the 1930s reinstates the photograph's evidential power in the classification of the Weimar Republic that was felt at the time of its production.

The section *Mortality* includes examples of the use of photography to distil characteristics of death by mediating the corpse through aesthetics whilst also alluding to methods of clinical observation. References to scientific modes of recording and examination are present in the work of Andres Serrano's *The Morgue* (1991) and Gwen Akin and Alan Ludwig's lavish platinum prints of body parts preserved in the collection of the Mütter Museum. This fascination with marginalised subject-matter challenges traditional categorisations and representations of the dead, by using a language which evokes the sublime. Photography was used to commemorate the dead in Victorian post-mortem and memorial portraits (1853–1905). These portraits obscure the reality of death as well as commemorating it. The photograph becomes a substitute for the lost object of desire, and identifies the corporeality of the dead through the visual experience of the living. A sense of mortality is also evident in one of the first X-rays ever made, by Wilhelm von Roentgen (c. 1895), which reveals

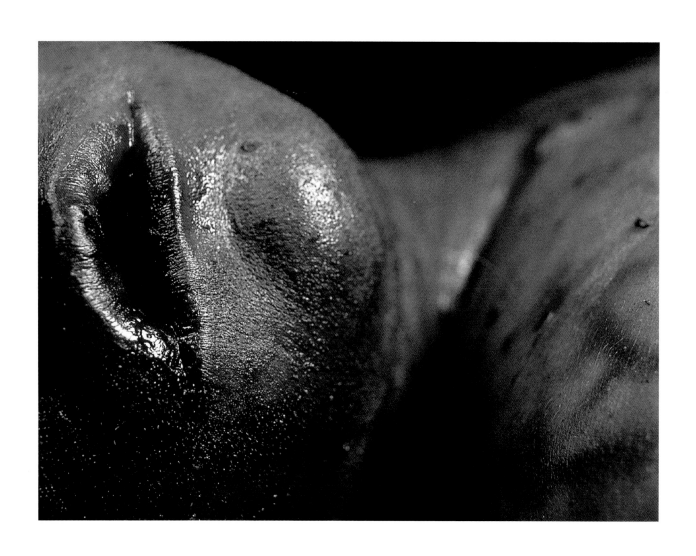

Andres Serrano

The Morgue (Death by Drowning II)
1992

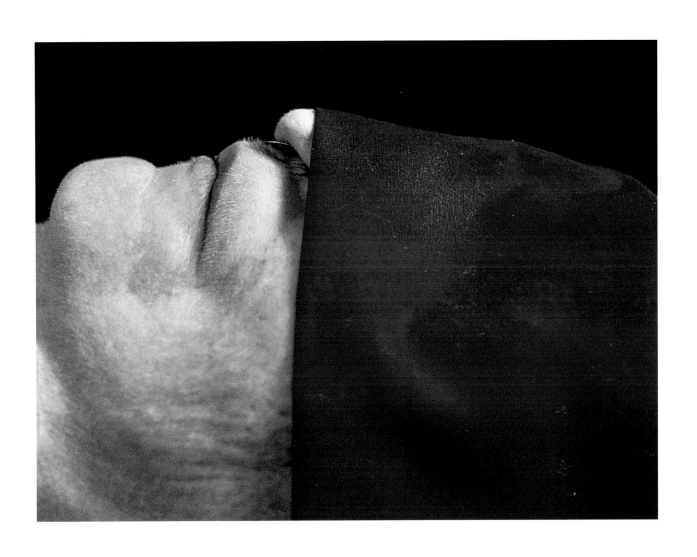

Andres Serrano

The Morgue (Infectious Pneumonia)

1992

Memorial photograph
date unknown

Gwen Akin & Allan Ludwig

Sliced Face #2

1985

the skeleton beneath the skin. Framed in this section, such scientific images become a form of memento mori.

The sentimental currency of the snapshot, usually located within the family album, is intensified when appropriated by the media to illustrate news items of crime. Family photographs of murder victims taken from the archive of *The Daily Herald* (1935–62) resonate with the morbidity of a public fascination which thrives on the spectacle of the pathological. Their emotional charge relies on the pathos and sentimentality associated with the images' original context.

Some of the photographs of the dead in this category reveal, through cropping and the use of drapery and colour, an unexpected beauty in bodies which have been medically and forensically inspected. The aesthetic mediation of the corpse transforms it from an object of fear and repulsion into a source of sublime fascination. The bringing of images of death into the realm of aesthetics challenges the clinical response to pathological subject matter, causing our perceptions of death to slip between the categories of both art and science.

In the nineteenth century, photography was perceived as what Fox-Talbot described as "the pencil of nature". *The Culture of Nature* presents ideas and images of the natural world which are mediated by culture. Many of these photographs derive their logic from categories determined by Natural History. Karl Blossfeldt combined this scientific method with a metaphysical approach to typology, believing "... (at a time when Darwin's ideas had begun to be popularly absorbed) that fundamental principles of structure – of survival – lay hidden in the natural world".[14] In his plant studies, details of plants, flowers and seedpods are abstracted into highly decorative, almost architectural forms. Blossfeldt's systematic approach, combining both science and aesthetics, typifies the questioning of nature's independence as an autonomous entity existing outside the confines of language. The influence of culture on nature can also be seen in photographs and formats appropriated from natural history books in the work of, for example, Cor Dera. In this context, Dera's allusion to scientific schemes for the purpose of comparative study evokes more exotic and romantic responses to the natural world. Biological engineering and the manufacture of nature appear in the work of certain artists and photographers who have used both natural and artificial means to generate new plant forms. Such subtle interventions present a problematic understanding of nature as a mediated entity; the work of Joan Fontcuberta and Chris Bucklow, for example, configures nature as an artificial, and even fictitious category.

Edward Fox's *The Anatomy of Foliage* (1864–5) was intended, on one level, simply as reference material for artists. However, his contextual and comparative studies use time as a variable for description, a

Murder victims: England, Scotland, Wales.
The Daily Herald Archive
1935–62

technique also present in the studies of animal locomotion by Eadweard Muybridge, in which images are multiplied and ordered through chronophotography. Muybridge uses time to measure the movement of animal bodies through space. Ironically, his record of a bird of prey in flight (1872–85) slips between the gridded backdrop of the physiological experiment and the trees of the enclosure. Nature is doubly encoded, as manufactured product of science and as spectacle, witnessed in the studies of birds and animals made within the artificial environment of the zoological garden.

Fontcuberta's *Herbarium* (1982–5) presents "hyper-real" plant specimens made from industrial waste. Nature in this instance becomes the detritus of culture. Plants hover ambiguously between reality and fiction. Again, the language of another system is used to substantiate the illusion of "truth" through the bi-nomial system of classification developed in the taxonomies of Carl Linnaeus in the eighteenth century. Fontcuberta exaggerates the evolutionary process of nature in his construction of hybrid forms, whilst mocking the classificatory methods associated with scientific knowledge. Chris Bucklow takes the concept of hybridity a stage further by experimenting with the genetic structure of plants, confusing the nature/culture dialectic. His work revives the study of the hereditary mechanisms of plants through artificial pollination by the Augustinian monk Johann Gregor Mendel in 1856, which pre-dated the Darwinian classification of the natural world.

In the section *The Everyday*, simple documents bring to light details of unseen, marginalised or forgotten aspects of social spaces and public and private identities, using formal devices such as seriality and repetition. Photography cuts into the fabric of everyday life to show hidden details which prompt recognition of that which is familiar yet ignored: "the camera intervenes with the resources of its lowerings and liftings, its interruptions and isolations, its extensions and accelerations, its enlargements and reductions...[It] introduces us to unconscious optics, as does psychoanalysis to

Arne Svenson

Faggots

1994

43

Gillian Wearing

Signs that say what you want them to say and not
signs that say what someone else wants you to say
1992—93

Humphrey Spender
Mass Observation
1937—38

unconscious impulses".[15] In the work of Diane Arbus and Gillian Wearing, the social identity of the subject is undermined or confused by the allusions to this psychological dimension in the photographic presentation of the public self.

The documentary photographs of Humphrey Spender, commissioned as part of the Mass-Observation project in Bolton in 1937, were made in order to provide a social record of working class life in Britain during the 1930s, using anthropological methods which incorporated information from diaries produced by those who were being observed. Yet Spender does not use the typological format of anthropology for rendering his subject matter; it is, rather, the methods by which the photographic material is processed and organised which invest it with anthropological and ethnographic value. By contrast, Bernd and Hilla Becher use a more formal taxonomic method to order typologies of vernacular architecture in *Framework Houses — Wiesenstrasse 35, Siegen* (1970). The use of

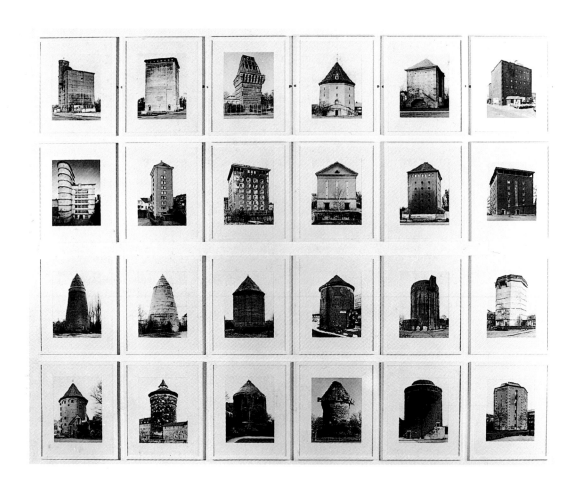

Boris Becker
Bunker Series
(Group 1 and 2)
1986—88

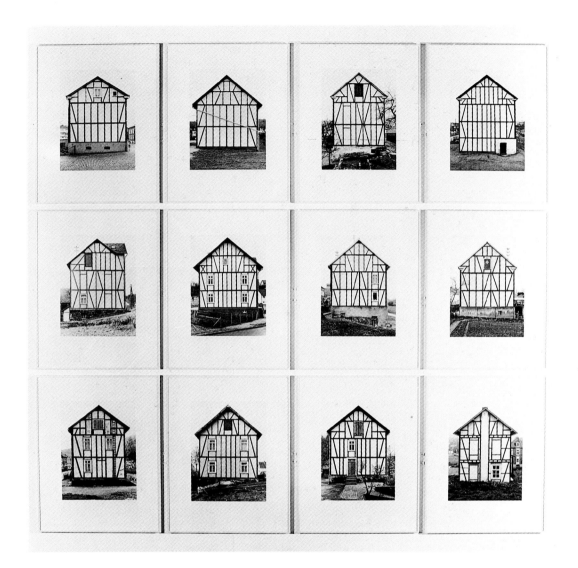

Bernd & Hilla Becher

Framework Houses-Wiesenstrasse 35, Siegen

1970

Eugene Atget

Hôtel de Lauzin

*c.*1900

Dan Graham
Highway Restaurant, Seattle
Bedroom Suite, "Model House", Staten Island, N.Y.
1974; 1967

Dan Graham
Diner on Highway, Staten Island, N.Y.
View from Window of Highway from Restaurant, Jersey City, N.J.
1967; 1969

typology as aesthetic does not remove the possibility of the image functioning as information in anthropological study: traces of the communities occupying such spaces offer glimpses into domestic life.

Ed Ruscha's serial photographs of parking lots and petrol stations echo the deadpan recordings of the Bechers. A more photojournalistic recording of the architectural metropolitan and suburban environment occurs in the photographs of Parisian architecture by Eugene Atget (*c.*1910), and in Dan Graham's recordings of American suburban diners and motel interiors, which suggest a continuation of Walker Evans' serial approach to the social landscape of consumer culture. Sol LeWitt's ordering of every domestic object in his apartment into gridded groups in his bookwork *Autobiography* (1980) shares the same concern to remove hierarchical value judgements as the Bechers' and Graham's recordings of the everyday social environment. Ruscha, Graham and

Sol LeWitt

Autobiography

1980

LeWitt's use of photographic seriality demonstrates the pervasive use of the grid by conceptual artists during the 1960s, which bears a relationship to Muybridge's use of the grid as a "scientific" measuring device, and its refusal of "background".[16]

The use of serial or archival methods of recording has many links with both early and late modernism. A number of photographs in this section demonstrate a clear set of aesthetic concerns, some of which resist the simple reduction of classification to an aesthetic and demonstrate a political and social awareness. Certain works, whilst apparently intrusive, seek to establish a clear dialogue between photographer, audience and subject. Although this category deals with the unseen or forgotten aspects of the everyday, it also highlights that which is deliberately lost or concealed, because of its power to contest familiar perceptions about people, places and things. The archival model established in the nineteenth century is configured in twentieth century work in terms of formalist aesthetic and ideological critique, shifting from an ambiguous relationship to those histories, to one which is more aware of the political dimensions of taxonomic discourse.

In terms of the photographic practices presented here, the formal characteristics and ideological legacies that seep through the two existing paradigms of photography as either an art or science are clearly entangled both visually and historically. Positivism's epistemological use of the photograph to map the terrain of the body and of culture relied on classificatory methods to organise perceptions of the photograph as document, and, equally, on the document to verify the method. Roland Barthes' description of the photograph as being either "mad or tame"[17] is a useful comparison in this context. The passivity associated with the photograph as evidence is subject to disruption through a recognition that its meaning is the product of relationships between cultural and historical forces that do not cling to its surface. *In Visible Light* is a gesture towards a historical method of understanding some of those histories.

Ed Ruscha
Thirtyfour Parking Lots
1967

1 For example, Charles Darwin's *The Expression of the Emotions in Man and Animals*, J. Murray, London, 1872, incorporated photographs by pictorialist photographer Oscar Rejlander, with material from Duchenne de Boulogne's *Mecanisme de la Physionomie Humaine*, V. J. Renouard, Paris, 1862

2 During 1991–2 I catalogued Dammann's album in the photography collection at the Victoria and Albert Museum, London. This material evoked the fascination I had with a number of contemporary photographic practices which explored classification from different perspectives, and which were concerned with a similar archival arrangement of their subject

3 The various factors involved in the visualisation of knowledge can only be activated in a restricted way through the exhibition; however, the relationships between images and the institutional uses of photography and classification have been the focus of a number of writings since the early 1980s. The social and cultural history of photography during the last fifteen years has done much to question the validity of uses of photography to represent and control the criminal, the sexually deviant, and the diseased body, as inscribed in nineteenth century institutions. See David Green, "The Veins of Resemblance: Photography and Eugenics", *The Oxford Art Journal*, 7.2, 1984; A. Sekula, "The Body and the Archive", *October* 36–39, 1986; John Tagg, *The Burden of Representation*, Macmillan, 1988; L. Cartwright, *Screening The Body – Tracing Medicine's Visual Culture*, Minnesota Press, 1995; S. Lalvani, *Photography, Vision, and the Production of Modern Bodies*, SUNY Press, 1996. What unites many of these texts is an approach to the relationships between photography and institutional power which owes much to methods of historical analysis deployed by Michel Foucault

4 Sekula raises the following question: "Can any connections be traced between the archival mode of photography and the emergence of photographic modernism? To what degree did self-conscious modernist practice accommodate itself to the model of the archive? To what degree did modernists consciously or unconsciously resist or subvert the model of the archive, which tended to regulate the individual photographer to the status of a detail worker, providing fragmentary images for an apparatus beyond his of her control?" "The Body and the Archive" (revised version) in R. Bolton, (ed.), *The Contest of Meaning*, MIT Press, 1989, pp. 374 – 375

5 Douglas Crimp, "The Museum's Old, the Library's New Subject", *On the Museum's Ruins*, MIT Press, 1993, p. 78

6 S. Greenblatt, "Resonance and Wonder", in I. Karps and S.D. Levine (ed.), *Exhibiting Cultures - The Poetics and Politics of Museum Display*, Smithsonian Institution Press, 1991, p. 42

7 Andre Malraux, "Museum Without Walls", *The Voices of Silence*, Doubleday and Co., 1953

8 S. Stewart, *On Longing – Narratives of the Miniature, the Gigantic, the Souvenir, The Collection*, Duke University Press, 1993, pp. 137–8

9 Douglas Crimp, "On the Museums Ruins", in Hal Foster (ed.), *The Anti-Aesthetic — Essays on Postmodern Culture*, Bay Press, 1983.

10 H.W. Diamond, "On the Application of Photography to the Physiognomic and Mental Phenomena of Insanity", *The Photographic Journal*, No. 3, July 1856, p. 88

11 Showalter, E., *The Female Malady — Women, Madness, and English Culture 1830–1980*, Virago Press, 1985, p. 84

12 Ibid, p. 87

13 John Tagg, "A Means of Surveillance: The Photograph as Evidence in Law", *The Burden of Representation*, Macmillan, 1988, p. 80

14 David Elliott, "Introduction", *Karl Blossfeldt Photographs*, Museum of Modern Art Oxford, 1978, p. 4

15 Walter Benjamin, "The Work of Art in the Age of Mechanical Reproduction", *Illuminations*, Fontana, 1973, p. 239

16 For a discussion of the grid in modernism, see Rosalind Krauss's essay on the grid in Rosalind Krauss, *The Originality of the Avant Garde and Other Modernist Myths*, M.I.T. Press, 1986

17 Roland Barthes, *Camera Lucida, Reflections on Photography*, 1980, Editions du Seuil, pp. 117–119

Eugene Atget

Boutique Louis XVI Quai Bourbon No. 8926

c. 1900

Ordering Others: Photography, Anthropologies and Taxonomies

Elizabeth Edwards

This short essay looks at the ways in which different bodies of nineteenth century anthropological material connect with various levels of taxonomic activity, both within and beyond anthropology. The way that photography functioned at the intersection of anthropological and taxonomic discourses in the nineteenth century demonstrates both the complexity and ambiguity of taxonomic desires in relation to its scientific, anthropological use, and to the fluidity of the photographic image. I hope to position them in terms of the affective tone of general ideas, and how they become concrete taxonomies.

The political and ideological arguments embedded in the conflation of scientific and photographic naturalism in the presentation of observable fact have long been recognised in writings about photography, the body and surveillance.[1] The focus of this text is on the different scientific procedures involved in the production of anthropological information, assumed or naturalised, within this process. The photograph is central to these discursive forms, which were presented as essential mechanisms of truth not only in anthropology, but within other meta-narratives of justification and value outside science.[2] These mechanisms have often been situated in Foucaultian terms – that is, in terms of surveillance, power and domination, within which anthropological photography is seen as a medium of instrumental power. Such elements are, however, entwined with the procedures of producing scientific data, scientific demonstration, and particularly the precise role of photography within them as they relate to taxonomy.

Anthropology during the nineteenth century was a coming together of many different lines of enquiry into the physical and cultural origins of the human race. There were anthropological concerns within, for instance, philology, anatomy, archaeology and religion, and different national emphases emerged within the general anthropological paradigm.[3] Scientific practice was also changing rapidly, with increasing professionalisation and the rise of recognisably modern laboratory conditions. Enquiry into the physical and cultural nature of the human species was formed through the delineation and elaboration of human difference. Taxonomy operated in this context as a central and unifying concept.

Beyond its base in the biological sciences, taxonomic activity should also be understood in the broader socio-economic contexts of the late nineteenth century – colonial expansion, mass movements of populations and the emancipation of slave and tied peasant populations. These should also be linked, in their turn, to evolutionary thinking, social progress and early modernist thought, all of which indicated a world and a human species in flux. These elements led to complex intersections of various definitions of the self and the "other", of inclusion and exclusion, and to a concern with roots and historical explanation, all of which functioned dialectically with the practice of ordering the human species and its cultures. Anthropology became one of the dominant discourses of explanation, embracing historically-based and biologically determined notions of culture, grounded in a comparative taxonomic method, the apparent unity of which was moulded by the discursive fields through which it was mapped. The morphological conceptualisation of the body in terms of its visible structure thus provided points of entry for other moral and cultural taxonomies which related back dialectically to the observer. The photographic mapping of the body contained a moral dimension which had a double, inter-related taxonomic agenda. This agenda was concerned with both creating and sustaining the social, economic, political and aesthetic practices which comprised the complex system of social knowledge within which these images operated.

In the history of science, much has been written on the instrument as an extension of the senses. The photographic apparatus was one of these instruments. The role of photography was to create "virtual witnesses" of scientific observation, and of the creation of scientific fact such as taxonomies. Through its immutability of inscription yet mutability of meaning, the photograph was integral to this complex, multi-layered symbiotic discourse. Whilst photography can be included within the mimetic structures which were used increasingly in nineteenth century science,[4] Its precise use at the intersections of photographic naturalism and scientific integrity suggests it belongs to different, but inter-related, micro-structures of visibility.

Thus those photographs used to create information through which the taxonomic process could be furthered can be distinguished from those which were more "demonstrational" in intention. Professor T.H. Huxley's and John Lamprey's anthropometric systems are concerned with the production of comparable data for analytical and classificatory purposes. Both systems were premised on the notion that quantifiable data could be read off the photographic image itself. In 1869 Lamprey published a system of measurement which posed the body against a backdrop divided into two inch squares by means of silk threads:

John Lamprey
Anthropometric
Study
Malayan Male
c.1868

By means of such photographs, the anatomical structure of a good academy figure or model of six feet can be compared with a Malay of four feet eight in height; and study of all those peculiarities of contour which are so distinctly observable in each group, is greatly helped by this system of perpendicular lines.[5]

In the same year Huxley, the distinguished biologist and champion and populariser of Darwinian theory, in his capacity as President of the Ethnological Society, devised a more complex scheme for the Colonial Office for the "formation of a systematic series of photographs of the various races of men comprehended within the British Empire".[6] Huxley was already closely involved with anthropology at this date,[7] and was concerned with the production of systematic anthropological data for taxonomic analysis:

Great numbers of ethnological photographs already exist but they lose much of their value from not being taken upon a uniform and well-considered plan. The result is that they are rarely either measurable or comparable with one another.

Huxley consequently responded to the Colonial Office's request with a detailed list of instructions for the visual recording and rendering of bodies, which were circulated to colonial governors and, through them, to photographers commissioned in the colonies.[8]

Both Lamprey and Huxley's systems use classic poses of the body for anatomical purposes: full face and profile, full length and half length, with emphasis on the delineation of characteristics (especially those of crania). The subjects were photographed in strong, even light, and isolated in shallow space against a plain background which projected the figure visually. Huxley's system used a measuring rod rather than a grid. Like Lamprey's system, the intention was to be able to read comparable taxonomic data off the image even when it was linked to statistical data, in at least sufficient detail to make a classificatory judgement.[9] Both systems are overt expressions of the positivist concentration on the "mathematicisation of empirica", and the related notion that images, like graphs, could work without text and become a controlled lexical space.[10] What is interesting is that Huxley's instructions appear to have been carried out to the letter only where coercive power was strongest, in prisons, such as those at Breakwater, Natal, South Africa, or the Malay Straits Settlement. It would also appear that, contrary to common assumption, the production of anthropological images, although remaining firmly within overall power relationships, was, to an extent, a negotiated process. A number of colonial Governors reported back that they were unable to comply with the request from the Colonial Office and Huxley because of local resistance to being photographed "in a state of total nudity" and the Governors' unwillingness to interfere with either the local colonial status quo or indigenous sensibilities. It was within this context that we begin to see the substitution of other forms of photographic inscription, such as commercially produced cartes de visite, as intellectually valid forms of representation of racial characteristics and taxonomic appropriateness. This is a point to which I will return.

Evidence of the production of information is also contained within more experimental methods, such as Galton's use of composite photography, which encompasses elements of both demonstration and proof. Galton's composite photographs constitute "lived concepts" – embodied or concrete ideas developed to render the unseen or non-existent empirically: in other words, a taxonomic essence within a dialectic of the visible and invisible. These ideas were most forcefully expressed in anthropometric and composite photography and had a profound influence, establishing a broad aesthetic of "scientific reference" which informed less structured photographic styles.

However, the mutability of photographic possibilities is underlined by the way in which images illustrating evolutionary or Darwinian monogenist arguments that man was a single but diversified species (and thus mutable) are stylistically indistinguishable from scientific reference photographs made precisely to demonstrate the opposite; for instance, the photographs made by Agassiz in Brazil in 1865[11] to demonstrate the immutability of species within a polygenist discourse which argued that the many races of humankind were separate and immutable species. Evidence of this taxonomic slippage of photographic styles themselves, where one set of meanings is privileged and others are suppressed, can be found in the shape of anthropological photographic collections in archives and museums throughout Europe and America.

The value of the production and presentation of taxonomic data depended on the photograph's role as what Latour has termed "the immutable mobile". This meant the transferring of inscriptions of information and experiences through space and time to different spheres of interpretation without any translation or transcription of the original rendering.[12] It was the creation of "immutable mobiles" that interested both Huxley and Lamprey – the idea that taxonomic data could be moved from a site of observation and inscription to a site of analysis without being corrupted. This enabled the anthropologist to become a "virtual witness" to "scientific fact" through the photographic image.

Charles Darwin
Plates 3 and 6 from *The Expression of the Emotions in Man and Animals*
J. Murray, London, 1873

Another procedure involved the use of photographs to demonstrate an argument which had already been arrived at scientifically.[13] Such a case is Darwin's use, in his book *The Expression of Emotions in Man and Animals* (1872), of Duchenne's photographs from *Mécanisme de la Physionomie Humaine ou analyse electrophysiologique de l'expression des passions* (1862), made by Adrien Tournachon, Nadar's younger brother. This is a classic example of the photograph as "immutable mobile". The original photographic data is accepted by another scientist and used to demonstrate his thesis. Immutability and objectivity were stressed by Darwin in his introduction:

> All these photographs [Duchenne's] have been printed by Heliotype process and the accuracy of the copy is thus guaranteed.[14]

Juxtaposed with Duchenne's images is a series of photographs taken by Oscar Rejlander in order for Darwin to demonstrate his hypothesis. The theatricality of Rejlander's figure-studies should not necessarily be seen as unscientific. It relates, rather, to a growing trend in nineteenth century laboratory practice to replicate the actualities of the physical, empirically experienced world in controlled conditions which allowed for their analysis. The presentation of a re-enactment did not necessarily invalidate the value of the image as scientific data in ways the interventionist notions of "pose" imply. All taxonomy relied on the recording of precise visual material presented to the camera. While the deeper, more naturalistic picture-plane encompasses a classical rather than scientific aesthetic, Rejlander's images function as demonstration rather than as morphological data. Significantly, both Duchenne and Rejlander were interested in the aesthetic potential of the scientific photograph.[15] This linked them to realist ideas of fine art and the aesthetic representation of expression, pointing to another kind of taxonomic slippage.[16] Yet these different forms of re-enactment – either the electronically stimulated or the dramatically figured – constitute, through a double mimetic effect, allowable demonstrations within Darwin's evolutionary and taxonomic reading of the emotions.[17]

The third function of photography which we should distinguish is its use in the broad confirmation of existing taxonomic readings. It is the Dammann album *Anthropologisch-Ethnologisches Album in Photographien* which most clearly expresses the currency of images within taxonomic thinking. Dammann's album is, in many ways, the most complex, even if its aims are somewhat ill-defined in intellectual terms. Dammann was a Hamburg photographer who, in addition to producing in his own studio images of "scientific reference", which used the aesthetic formations of "serious scientific intent", also produced and disseminated copies of photographs of "anthropological" interest on behalf of the *Berliner Gesellschaft für Anthropologie, Ethnologie und Urgeschichte* (BGAEU). Published between 1873 and 1874 the *Album* comprises ten sections of five folios each, containing in all over six hundred photographs.[18]

It would be a mistake to classify this *Album* within an overly determined Darwinian model. Whilst there is an emphasis which may draw its basis from the analytical construct of *naturvölken,* at the same time it allows the possibility of differently nuanced analytical paradigms. Thus it might be argued that it is not so much a taxonomy, in scientific terms, as a series of illustrations onto which precise taxonomic readings could be projected. In Germany, Darwinism represented only one element of contemporary scientific concern. There were many non-scientific considerations which influenced opinions on evolutionary theory, especially those concerned with social organisation, nationalism and the rise of the modern German state.[19] Perhaps it is therefore significant that the shape of the popular English edition of the *Album,* the *Races of Men* (1875) is more strongly Darwinian, for by 1870 Darwinian ideas had saturated the British popular imagination.[20] The progression through *The Races of Men* from the "civilised" Europeans on the first page[21] to Australians, Melanesians and Micronesians on the last makes a clear evolutionary statement. The *Album* itself lacks such precise taxonomic incision. Its closure of meaning is not complete.

Nevertheless, the rituals of scienticity (those subjective cultural actions of science) resonate throughout. The images are arranged in a grid, suggesting ordered scientific presentation and echoing the anthropometric grid. But the album also suggests the grid of a photographic album, with its arrangement of images of personal experience. Like the photographs sent in response to requests from the Colonial Office and Huxley, the *Album* and *The Races of Men* contain a wide range of images, pointing to a complex assumption of taxonomic appropriateness. Included are some of Lamprey's anthropometric images, Gustav Fritsch's photographs of South African "types", with plain backgrounds, a rigid scientific focus and a shallow picture plane, and commercial cartes de visite. The latter function ambiguously, as visual dialects of studio portraiture – props and naturalistic lighting – merge with scientific references inscribed on the isolated body. A mixture of geographical and evolutionary or progressive taxonomies interweaves through the whole *Album*, creating both a

Carl and Frederick Dammann
Ethnographical Photographic Gallery of the various Races of Men
Trüber, London, 1875

social continuum and a conflation of photographic practices, together naturalised within the arrangements of the material.[22] While this eclecticism was criticised by some contemporaries who supported the project, notably A. Bastian of the BGAEU,[23] their critique was based on the taxonomic confusion of differing anthropological interests and their perceived photographic manifestations, rather than on types of photographs *per se*. The British anthropologist, E.B. Tylor, reviewing the *Album* in *Nature* in 1876, points to this key weakness in taxonomic terms, which clearly illuminates the arbitrariness of categories. "The plan on which the portraits are arranged is mainly geographical, exact race-division being, from the nature of the case, impracticable". Yet at the same time he described it as "one of the most important contributions ever made to the science of man".[24] He is caught between photographic realism and scientific method.[25]

Taxonomic intentions do, however, emerge in the treatment of some images. Some copy negatives were overpainted in order to eliminate the subject's background and cultural references. This re-touching contains the image firmly within the frame reference. However ambiguous in stylistic form, the images are translated from a vernacular to a scientific genre, focusing the viewer's attention on the body of the subject as presented in socio-political taxonomic spaces. The juxtaposing of "cultural" and "physical" images in the Dammann albums mirrors the slippage between the scientifically produced and the scientifically perceived.

The Dammann album also raises other issues regarding the translation of images between different visual forms. The German *Album* and the popular *Races of Men* both contain anthropometric-style images from Gustav Fritsch, the German anatomist and anthropologist. The oppressive repetition of photographic style comes across strongly in the nine folios of between sixteen and eighteen images each in the large *Album*. Yet "truth" in these photographs was constructed precisely through their repetition. A visual rhythm stressed the similarity of type within the paradigmatic cultural notion of "Bushman" people or "Zulu" people. These images form the basis of the engravings

which had appeared in Fritsch's atlas *Die Eingeborenen Sud-Afrikas*, published in Breslau in 1872. In the preface he stresses the truthfulness of his engravings as being based in their having been traced off photographs, which were themselves traced by light on the photographic plate. Photographic pedigree authenticates anthropological validity. It is precisely this argument concerning the veracity of translation from the photographic plate that Darwin uses. It should be seen as an attempt to sustain the mimetic and immutable qualities of the photograph in a non-photographic method of reproduction.

Prince Roland
Bonaparte
Peaux Rouge
1883

A similar ambiguity regarding the intersection of race, culture, photographic inscription and photographic style emerges in Bonaparte's photographs: the *Peaux Rouge* series of portraits of Omaha people made in Paris at the Jardin d' Acclimatation in 1883, where the subjects were "performing" their culture for popular entertainment.[26] Whilst the series was related to broader cultural concerns on one level, Bonaparte's work comes strongly out of the medical discourses and informed French anthropology under Broca and Quatresfuges, where a strictly Darwinian model was regarded as only one amongst a range of transformist theories.[27] The images all contain strong scientific references: all are full face and profile, with culture displayed through the subjects' "full dress" of buckskins, beads, feathers and abalone shell. Yet the spatial dynamic and the paraphernalia of vernacular photography speak to other visual genres, creating uncertainty and ambiguity. It inserts the historical specifics of the encounter into the taxonomic discourse with a fracturing force. As such, it echoes the taxonomic uncertainties which resonate in the Huxley project and the Dammann albums, through the juxtaposition of styles and the conflated discourses of the folio arrangement.

It is difficult to assess to how these images were actually used, and the extent to which they were an active part of the debate, as opposed to being absorbed effortlessly as confirmation. Despite the effort invested in the making and collecting of images such as those made for or by Duchenne, Huxley and Lamprey, and, later, the intentions which shaped their archiving and documentation, the images remain an end in themselves. Galton's photographs, on the other hand, are actively engaged with, in a discursive analysis. They "revealed" the invisible or non-existent constructed photographically. The *Album* can be seen as a visual reference of other theoretical perspectives in mid-nineteenth century anthropology. Its eclectic absorption of images and isolated pictorial elements also suggests the conceptual linking meta-narrative through which different visual dialects and agendas are absorbed into an overt taxonomic structure, in which contradictory desires and anxieties were variously suppressed, legitimated or rationalised. Only the culturally-delineated contexts of viewing separated the "arduous disciplinary gaze" from a voyeuristic, flâneur-like browsing of images.

I have considered the nature of the Dammann *Album* at some length since its eclecticism illustrates the encompassing, yet ambiguous, nature of such taxonomies. Photographic taxonomies of peoples were re-figured, through time and space, from a series of specific scientific questions to a series of generalised statements. Even within their own periods, the images underwent transformations, accruing new meanings. For instance, one of the frontal half-lengths taken of Khoisan prisoners at Breakwater Prison, Natal by Lawrence and Selkirk according to Huxley's instructions, was reproduced by the same photographers and vignetted in the mode of the European portrait (perhaps to obliterate the oppressive machinery of taxonomy), for Dr. Wilhelm Bleek, who had, at the same time, been instrumental in the making of the original anthropometric images.[28]

Paradoxically, as a culturally-based anthropology emerged, the legacy of nineteenth century taxonomic agendas became more insidious. In contrast to the overt objectification of anthropometric practices, everyday taxonomic assumptions in the consumption of "cultural" images at once made natural and obscured discursive activity to such an extent that an "ethnographical" or "anthropological" reading of such photographs was, arguably, the only possible reading. The systemic naturalising of scientific taxonomic notions of race and culture was even more marked at a popular level. Publications such as the fortnightly magazine *The Living Races of Mankind* (1902–3) and, later, *Women of All Nations* reproduced their taxonomic arguments culturally naturalised through the realist appearance of the photographs which adorned almost every page. "Ethnographic" became a catch-all classification for any image with non-European figurative subject matter, regardless of specific scientific or social intent. The inherent ambiguities are illustrated further in the "ethnographic" material in Benjamin Stone's collection. This encompasses his own snapshots from his travels, and commercially and scientifically produced photographic material. Read in terms of his whole collection, it appears to function as an ethnographic counterpoint to the British folklore material of his National Photographic Archive. Theories of primitive survival made the European peasantry and rural custom the crucial link between modern European civilisation and its primitive and savage past. Such theories functioned in the same self-referential and self-defining ways as more morphological taxonomic structures of non-European peoples had, establishing discourses of cultural origins and progress.[29] However, the role of these ideas within the British context was presented as inclusive and culturally formative for the British nation, whereas the primitive of the ethnographic was placed on a different primitivist trajectory. Such an exclusive taxonomic paradigm rendered it culturally impossible for images of non-European peoples to be viewed other than in broad ethnographic terms, as generalised culture rather than historically-specific people.

Photographs (published and unpublished), the archive and the taxonomies which created it and which it itself sustained, could all be read as "textual deposits" of scientific thinking and procedure. Evidence is subsumed in the presentation of scientific fact, and then rejected as it is no longer convincingly valid. It is precisely the lack of validity with which nineteenth century taxonomies and colonial power structures are now viewed which has opened up a space for their critique. This critique has come not only in scientific, and often non-photographic form, but through a re-engagement with taxonomic aesthetics, through a confrontation with scientific "textual deposits". The nineteenth century positivist view of science and photography in all its complex forms constituted images as a quantifiable window on nature. It is precisely this element within taxonomic structures that is disrupted by contemporary staged and manipulated photographs, particularly by those artists associated with post-modern contemporary art.[30] Such artists use the camera not as an instrument to record or reveal either essentialist or existential truths, but rather as a "cerebral tool for the manufacture of deceit",[31] thus challenging, fracturing or inverting taxonomic assumptions. The hybrid illusions and serendipitous connections in these works make no pretence of relating to the intact world of, for instance, Huxley's taxonomies. The borders which characterise taxonomic thinking and the sites of their making no longer pertain. They have been replaced by the compositional principles of merger and takeover, hybridity and ambiguity. This is not merely a dichotomy between art and science; for science, understanding, feeling and expression are linked through their broad, abstract, intangible yet unifying cultural formations.[32] Rather, it is a realignment of authorities. A re-drawing of the boundaries of descriptive possibility within anthropology[33] has suggested an increasing confluence between contemporary anthropology and contemporary art as areas within which cultural meanings are made and debated.[34] Further, both have *specific* sites of investigation – cultural reproduction, gender, memory – in common. These sites are used for tracking, representing and articulating the effects of "difference" – the boundaries between observer and observed and, by implication, taxonomical spaces.

Contemporary artists have explored the taxonomic spaces both inside the photographic frame and outside in the spaces of consumption; for as we have seen, meaning resides in the discourse between the two. A shift has occurred from "immutable mobiles" transmitting "factual inscription" over space and time (the focus of an historical study of Dammann or Lamprey) to an interplay of all that is mutability and flux, and all that consciously defies traditional notions of taxonomy.

Dave Lewis's work engages with spaces such as the Royal Anthropological Institute and the Museum of Archaeology and Anthropology at the University of Cambridge, which produced and reproduced visual taxonomic meanings, and re-inserts the emblematic classified subject into physical space. The use of the fish-eye lens with combined images and reflections sets up overtly photographic interventions in these spaces. His images stress the role of photography in constructing traditional anthropological discourse. Ken Lum inverts the relation between the subject and the

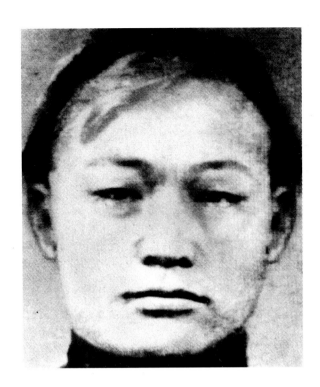

Nancy Burson
Mankind
1983–84

Dave Lewis
Haddon Photographic Collection, Cambridge
University Museum of Anthropology and
Ethnography
1995

Ken Lum

Mohammed And The Totems

1991

viewer's expectation, through disruptive juxtapositions focused on cultural/ethnic assumptions. His images, such as *Mohammed And The Totems* (1991) draw to the surface and exorcise latent taxonomic cultural baggage from the past, and construct a different, oppositional taxonomy.

Nancy Burson's composite photographs, for example *Mankind* (1983–5), examine the ways in which taxonomies have erased specific identities. She not only merges individual portraits, as Galton did, but uses scanning technology to merge individual features into one portrait, using traditional "types", children with cranio-facial deformities and dolls' eyes. The imaginary and the real fuse, questioning the whole status of scientific naturalism and the scientific paradigms within which it operates. Although stylistically and technically reminiscent of Galton's composites, Burson's images work from the notion of the impossibility of "type".

The subversive elements in these artworks depend not on rejecting or altering in a straightforward sense, but on using taxonomic concepts or materials in conjunction with concepts and references totally foreign to them, reappropriating spaces organised for very different agendas of sociocultural reproduction. All this work points to the flexible and transitory nature of taxonomies which deal with the characteristics of humankind. However, even when superseded, ideas leave their scientific deposits, and these remain the tools with which we can interrogate our own taxonomic assumptions, and the procedural agencies which both make and sustain them.

1   For instance John Tagg, *The Burden of Representation: Essays on Photographies and Histories*, Macmillan, London, 1988; David Green "Veins of Resemblance: Photography and Eugenics" *Oxford Art Journal*, 1985, 7 (2):3–16 and Alan Sekula "The Body and the Archive" in Richard Bolton (ed.), *The Contest of Meaning*, MIT Press, Cambridge, Mass, 1989, pp. 342–388

2   See Green, ibid: 6; Elizabeth Edwards "'Photographic Types': The Pursuit of Method' *Visual Anthropology*, 1990, 3: 235–258

3   Anthropology in the late twentieth century remains a fluid discourse broadly grounded in shared theoretical, methodological and subject concerns

4   The late nineteenth century saw an increasing trend for replication in laboratory practice which attempted to reproduce natural phenomena, with all their complexity, in the laboratory. Mimetic tradition was part of a continuing dialogue between general theories and particular demonstrations of natural phenomena (see P. Galison and A. Assmus, "Artificial Clouds, Real Particles" pp. 226–227 in D. Gooding, T. Pinch and S. Schaffer (eds.), *The Uses of Experiment*, Cambridge University Press, Cambridge, pp. 225–274). The use of photography as material manifestation in anthropological taxonomies might be seen, therefore, as a confluence of these two traditions: the analytic and the mimetic. The fascination with mimesis is also a distinguishing feature of popular culture, tied to the whole culture of vision and spectacle. Nevertheless one should not assume undifferentiated applications of mimesis

5   J. Lamprey, "On a Method of Measuring Human Form for Students of Ethnology", *Journal of the Ethnological Society*, 1869, N.S. 1:84–85

6   This project would appear to emulate *The Peoples of India* which had begun to appear in 1868 and aroused favourable interest amongst anthropologists and in the government

7   Much later, in 1889, Huxley wrote to A.C. Haddon, a Dublin zoologist-fast-becoming Cambridge anthropologist: "I know no department of natural science more likely to reward a man who goes into it thoroughly than anthropology. There is an immense amount to be done in the science pure and simple, and it is one of those branches of inquiry which brings one into contact with the great problems of humanity in every direction. I have dabbled in it a good deal and I should have liked nothing better than to give myself up to it" (Quoted in A. Hingston Quiggen, *Haddon the Headhunter*, Cambridge University Press, Cambridge, 1942 p. 93)

8   For a detailed account of this project see E. Edwards, "Photographic 'Types': The Pursuit of Method", *Visual Anthropology* 1990 3:235–258. In fact relatively few instances of the system, executed precisely, were forthcoming. Many colonial governors furnished the project with generic "types" and cartes-de-visite

9   For instance M.V. Portman's anthropometric portraits of Andaman Islanders drew on Lamprey's method. The measurements themselves were done on the subjects (and included heart rate, respiratory rate, temperature etc.), rather than read off the image as had been the intention with Lamprey's system. The photograph was a parallel form of morphological data, but also functioned as part of the

demonstration and proof to convince the viewer that textual explanations and numerical tabulations and reductions were not in error. See Christopher Pinney, "Colonial Anthropology and 'The Laboratory of Mankind' in C. Bayley (ed.), *The Raj: India and the British 1600 – 1942*, National Portrait Gallery, London, 1990, pp. 252–263, 285–286

10 Barbara Stafford, *Body Criticism: Imaging the Unseen in Enlightenment Art and Medicine*, MIT Press, Cambridge, Mass, 1991, pp. 469

11 Gwyniera Isaac, "Louis Agassiz's Photographs in Brazil: Separate Creations", *History of Photography* 1997 21(1): 3–11

12 Bruno Latour "Visualization and Cognition: 'Thinking with Eyes and Hands'", *Knowledge and Society*, 1986, 6:1–40

13 Arguably, of course, at a meta-level all taxonomies are "positions already arrived at", and thus all photographs presented and consumed within taxonomic discourses might be described as having a demonstrational function

14 Charles Darwin, *The Expression of the Emotions*, John Murray, London, 1873, p.25

15 There is an implied aesthetic dimension in Lamprey, who compared his photographs advantageously in their potential to represent "academy figures"

16 See R. Andrew Cuthbertson, "The Highly Original Dr. Duchenne" and Jean-François Debord "The Duchenne de Boulogne Collection in the Department of Morphology, l'École Nationale Supérieure des Beaux Arts", in Cuthbertson (ed.), *The Mechanism of Human Facial Expression*, Cambridge University Press, Cambridge, 1990, pp. 225–241, 242–256; Hugh C. Marles "Duchenne de Boulogne", *History of Photography* 1992, 16(4):395–396; Stephanie Spencer "O.G. Rejlander: Art Studies" in Mike Weaver (ed.) *British Photography in the Nineteenth Century: The Fine Art Tradition*, Cambridge University Press, Cambridge, 1989, pp. 121–132

17 Darwin's analysis includes a large amount of material on "the primitive stages of mankind" sent to him by colonial officers and settlers. Like photographs in Huxley's or Dammann's project (see below) it is a movement of information from the periphery to the centre, where it is absorbed into taxonomically sustained forms of knowledge

18 For details see Thomas Theye, "Wir wollen nicht glauben, sondern schauen. Zur Geschichte der ethnographischen Fotografie im deutschsprachigen Raum im 19. Jahrhundert" in Theye (ed.), *Der geraubte Schatten*, Münchner Stadtmuseum, Munich, 1989, pp. 70–72

19 Paul J. Weindling, "Darwinism in Germany". In David Kohn (ed.), *The Darwinian Heritage*, Princeton University Press, Princeton, 1985, pp. 685–698

20 There was also a small German "schools edition", see Thomas Theye, "Einige Neuigkeiten zu Leben und Werk der Brüder Carl Victor und Friedrich Wilhelm Dammann", *Mitteilungen aus der Museum für Völkerkunde, Hamburg* (forthcoming)

21 Where, significantly, the "type" British male is David Livingstone and the "type" German is Bismarck

22 The images deemed of "anthropological interest" were gathered by BGAEU from German expatriate communities across the world. They were then copied for the project by Dammann on behalf of BGAEU. See Theye, 1989

23 See Theye (forthcoming)

24 E.B. Tylor, "Dammann's Race-Photographs", *Nature* XIII Jan. 6 1876:184

25 The Huxley and Lamprey systems and the Damman project through the Berliner Gesellschaft should all be seen in the context of broader moves towards greater qualitative control of the collection and production of anthropological data, both physical and cultural. In 1874 the British Association for the Advancement of Science published a pocket sized book *Notes and Queries on Anthroplogy* which, through a series of suggested questions, effectively delineated the observations considered significant in gathering of information. A similarly intended list of instructions, *Rathschlägen für anthropologische Untersuchungen auf Expeditionen der Marine,* had appeared in Germany in 1872, followed in 1875 by *Anleitung zu wissenschaftlichen Beodbachtungen auf Reisen*, edited by Georg Neumayer, which included photographic instructions (see Theye, 1989:72,89). The taxonomic and photographic implications of such volumes are clear in that they established clearly articulated frameworks in which anthropological truths were to be made. Consequently, certain classes of information were privileged over others, and thus visualised

26 Such spectacles are beyond the scope of this essay but should be seen as part of the overall taxonomic discourse which defined and performed the exotic

27 See Nelia Dias, "Photographier et mesurer: les portraits anthropologiques", *Romantisme* 1994, 84:37– 49; P. Corsi, "Recent Studies on French Reactions to Darwin", In David Kohn (ed.), *The Darwinian Heritage*, Princeton University Press, Princeton, 1985, pp. 698–711

28 Bleek, a pioneer of Bushman ethnography, took the subject //Kabbo into his home to teach him [Bleek] about Bushman culture. The simple act of suppressing the scientific apparatus might be read as a step towards a more humanising image. For a full discussion of the making of these images see Michael Godby "Images of //Kabbo" in. P. Skotnes (ed.), *Miscast: Negotiating the Presence of the Bushmen*, University of Cape Town Press, Cape Town, 1996, pp. 115–127

29 See George Stocking, *Victorian Anthropology*, University of Wisconsin Press, Madison, 1987 pp. 162–163, 218–219; for a general account of the various taxonomic agendas involved with the study of British race and culture, see James Urry "Englishmen, Celts and Iberians: The Ethnographic Survey of the United Kingdom, 1892–1899" in *Before Social Anthropology: Essays on the History of British Anthropology*, Harwood Academic Press, Philadelphia, 1993, pp. 83–101

30 For instance Barbara Kruger and Cindy Sherman. See Douglas Crimp *On the Museum's Ruins*, MIT Press, Cambridge, Mass., 1993 (especially pp. 107–137)

31 In that the camera, rather than being used to record "truth", is used to give concrete realistic appearance to a series of critical interrelated intellectual ideas. Images are thus premised on the abstract rather than the physical and didactic

32 Barbara Stafford, *Body Criticism,* pp. 28–29, 469

33 See E. Edwards, "Beyond the Boundary: Ethnography and Photographic Expression" in M. Banks and H. Morphy (eds.), *Rethinking Visual Anthropology*, Yale University Press, London/New Haven, 1997, pp. 53–80

34 George Marcus and Fred Myers (eds.), "Introduction: The Traffic in Art and Culture" in *The Traffic in Culture: Refiguring Art and Anthropology*, University of California Press, Berkeley, 1995. They argue further (pp. 29–31) that art has appropriated anthropology as part of its own critical discourses, especially the notion of distinctive difference, which clearly has a taxonomic base. Conversely, the ethnographic avant-garde models itself on art. Contemporary art has rejected anthropology as a way to "know" culture by explicitly positioning it as flawed and limited, while appropriating anthropology's traditional space for "knowing culture". Yet within this space cultures are de-territorialised and circulated through a modern global system

Written on the Body

Abigail Solomon-Godeau

Just as simulacra seem to be poised to take over the world, it is all the more important to attempt to decipher them. Laura Mulvey[1]

In the past ten years or so, there has emerged a scholarly discourse concerned to investigate the unstable couplet vision/visuality. Somewhat divorced from earlier inquiries premised on perceptualist, existentialist or phenomenological models, recent work examines ways by which vision and visuality are variously shaped by psychic, social, cultural and historical determinations, an enquiry wholly at odds with older beliefs in an innocent or uncultured eye; to quote André Breton: "The eye exists in its savage state".[2] On the contrary, the gist of contemporary thinking on the subject proposes that there is no ocular innocence, much less a savage state of grace. The gaze, the look, the visual field are all conceived, to a greater or lesser extent, as being inscribed within a semiotic nexus of signs, language, and socialisation. Hal Foster's cogent differentiation between vision and visuality and the stakes in their investigation is useful here:

> Although vision suggests sight as a physical operation, and visuality sight as a social fact, the two are not opposed as nature to culture; vision is social and historical too, and visuality involves the body and the psyche. Yet neither are they identical: here, the difference between the terms signals a difference within the visual – between the mechanism of sight and its historical techniques, between the datum of vision and its discursive determinations – a difference, many differences, among how we see, how we are able, allowed or made to see, and how we see this seeing or the unseen therein.[3]

Prompted in part by the centrality of vision in the work of Jacques Lacan, and the no-less influential reflections of Michel Foucault, but equally encouraged by the (often unacknowledged) influence of feminist thought and its critique of ocularcentrism, much of this critical work attempts to map the mechanisms of desire as they form and inform the visual field. It is therefore significant that, even when reflecting on the psychic and cultural determinations of picture viewing, few of these books and articles concerned with the visual field traffic much with the notion of beauty. What might be called a discursive cleavage has occurred, such that discourses of beauty have become detached from their historical locations in philosophy, aesthetics and art making. Obviously the cultural site which now generates the most powerful and explicit discourses of beauty and desire is women's fashion magazines, but Hollywood film as well as other kinds of mass media have been equally important sites of such production.

Nevertheless, if beauty is now largely the redoubt of cultural conservatives, or perceived as belonging more appropriately to the realm of "commodity aesthetics",[4] the theorisation or analysis of desire – in its distinctly modern libidinalised sense – has become a central preoccupation throughout a wide range of disciplines and practices, within both the humanities and the social sciences. Desire of the subject, powers of desire, female desires, the forms of desire, desire in language, desire in looking, policing desire, tradition and desire, the obscure object of desire[5] – desire is a discursive field with an ever more extensive purview, whereas beauty, once the fetish of aesthetic philosophy, has largely been eclipsed by other concerns.

The discursive eclipse of beauty by desire in contemporary philosophical and aesthetic thought is, however, like any other tidal shift in *mentalités*, very much over-determined. In the case of art production, the replacement of beauty – *le beau* – as an aesthetic standard by other criteria is, itself, the legacy of modernist avantgardes. By challenging or jettisoning classical notions of beauty as an objective, unchanging and atemporal order or canon, modernist art practices did much to de-legitimise Beauty as a quasi-juridical entity. Alternatively, modernist movements effectively revised, relativised or subjectivised its terms. Outside of aesthetic discourse, where concepts of beauty and desire have conventionally and historically been understood to be implicated in each others' terms, these have usually been within the context of a discourse on Woman, or within a discourse of femininity, or in relation to the image of ideal femininity, imagined in certain kinds of aesthetic discourse to be itself co-terminus with the concepts of beauty and desire.[6]

An exception to this discursive cleavage is Francette Pacteau's *The Symptom of Beauty*.[7] It is her deceptively simple thesis that the attributive and projective act of designating beauty is as much shaped by unconscious mechanisms and drives as by cultural conventions. Which is to say that those acts of visual production and reception mobilising concepts of beauty and desire can be said to tap into both the imaginary and the symbolic order. Citing Freud's observation that "The love of beauty seems a perfect example of an impulse inhibited in its aim", hence a psychic formation forged and lodged in the unconscious, she reflects on tropes and figures for feminine beauty and reads them symptomatically. "I am interested," she writes, "in the psychical apparatus to which the beholder's eye is attached: that is to say, I am interested less in the contingent object of desire than the fantasy which frames it."[8] Unsurprisingly, her reading of a range of cultural artefacts – Renaissance love

E.J. Bellocq
Untitled (Storyville Portraits)
c.1912

poetry, nineteenth century novels and contemporary photographs – reveals that where feminine beauty (a fairly mutable entity throughout the centuries) is defined or described, what is ultimately at stake devolves on the requirements and aporias of masculine subjectivity. Hence, although beauty is a socially and culturally-defined set of tropes and conventions, there is, nonetheless, a fantasmatic component to the way beauty is imagined and articulated. And insofar as discourses of beauty have historically been patriarchal constructions, they are principally shaped by the terms of male subjectivity.

Studies such as Pacteau's build on a legacy of feminist work on representation inaugurated initially in psychoanalytic film theory and subsequently elaborated and/or revised by a quarter century of feminist scholarship and theory. Because feminist theory has sought to understand the relations between representation and the historical real, and given the ways in which concepts of beauty impact on women's lives, the discursive constellation beauty, desire, femininity and representation has been, in feminist theory and feminist art, an important area of investigation. When these investigations are further integrated with analyses of the gaze, or the politics of looking, it is clear that the stakes in these enquiries are anything but academic. If beauty is thus taken as an object of critical interrogation by feminism, and largely ignored in much work on vision and visuality, there is reason to think that

Baron Wilhelm von Gloedon
Untitled study of three young boys
c.1900

this is due to feminism's insistence on the material, as well as psychic, ramifications of the unequal ordering of sexual difference in contrast to a marked tendency, on the part of male theorists of visuality, to elide issues of sexual difference altogether. Accordingly, and in contrast to much recent vapourising around the topics of vision and visuality, Pacteau assumes that the subject's negotiation of sexual difference, and the unconscious fantasies that attend it, are necessarily and inescapably involved in all aspects of visual perception and reception, and these have real (and differing) consequences for male and female subjects. Moreover, as Jacqueline Rose proposed in a classic essay, the field of vision is traversed and disturbed by the vicissitudes of the instinct, the diversions of the aim, the contingency of desire.[9] If, for example, classical *canonic* conceptions of female beauty, from the Medici *Venus* to Ingres' *Venus Anadyomene*, require the suppression of both body hair and sex organs, there is no way to account for this outside of the psychoanalytic model of fetishism, which presumes that the female body is an (unconscious) locus of and for (male) castration fears. Taking into account their social, psychic and historical determinations, a critical consideration of beauty and desire as they are invoked, produced, or mobilised within representational and scopic regimes might well begin with the interrogatives "whose beauty?" and "whose desire?".

These questions are, to be sure, political rather than aesthetic ones, contradicting the assumption of universality that concepts of beauty have historically implied. Addressing these questions to the arty tableaux of Wilhelm von Gloeden, to E. J. Bellocq's enigmatic photographs of Storyville prostitutes, or to the far less artful fare of an anonymous pornographer makes clear, however, the difficulties which attend the task of "thinking" such over-freighted concepts as beauty and desire in some kind of relation to photography, whether it is a question of specific images or photography *sui generis*.

Consider, for example, Wilhelm von Gloeden's own orchestration of beauty and desire in *Untitled Study of Three Young Boys* (c.1900). Here, in semiotic collision, are the clashing codes of iconicity and indexicality, the latter term complicating, if not subverting, traditional discourses of desire and beauty that depend on idealist (and idealising) aesthetics. On the side of iconicity resides von Gloeden's photograph's status as picture and as aesthetic artefact. Also on the side of iconicity is its literal components – what it is of – and its formal organisation. These include its denotative elements (for example, naked boys, Mediterranean setting and "classical" props like the embroidered fabric and the Greek *oinochoe*). Connotative meanings too are on the side of iconicity: "Greek love", pederasty, an imagined and thus licit space for homoerotic desire, as well as various high-toned artistic and literary allusions (for example, academic poses and Arcadian themes). This particular iconography was long a staple of academic painting, and like so many art photographers before and after him, von Gloeden was obviously striving to appropriate literary and pictorial motifs for photography.[10]

Few observers, however, either in von Gloeden's epoch or our own, would likely find the youths in the photograph to be especially beautiful. On the other hand, there are many reasons to suppose that for von Gloeden himself, and for his substantial clientele, such youths were, indeed, objects of desire. In this respect, one might note that where the perception of beauty may well provoke the spectator's desire, conversely, desire has no intrinsic need of beauty, as is perfectly evident in the case of most industrially-produced pornography. Furthermore, the perception of beauty, as such, enters neither into the psychic mechanisms of voyeurism, nor into those of narcissism, both of which may be mobilised in the act of photographic reception. As Victor Burgin has commented "… the look from this position [the identification of the subject with the camera position] will shift between the poles of voyeurism and narcissism: in the former instance subjecting the other-as-object to an inquisitive and controlling surveillance, in which seeing is disassociated from being-seen; and in the latter effecting a dual identification with both the camera *and* the individual depicted."[11]

That said, a connoisseur of art photography might consider the photograph itself to be beautiful, in keeping with that aspect of modern aesthetics that detaches the beauty or ugliness of a work's nominal subject from the quality of a work *qua* work. There exists, then, the possibility that the picture itself, as material object, on shiny or matte paper, in sepia or black and white tones, is as much the object of desire as the youths who occupy its pictorial field. Indeed, photographic imagery does not so much lie on the surface of a photograph – as paint does on canvas or ink on paper – so much as it seems to inhere within it: the surface and the image are isomorphic and are perceptually insepa-rable. In this respect, and as Burgin additionally observes, "…identification need not be with any overt depicted 'content' whatsoever: if we bear in mind the *gestalt* orientation of the mirror-phase – its emphasis on surface and boundary – we can admit that a narcissistic investment may be made in respect of the very specular brilliance of the tightly-delineated photographic surface itself… Such fascination with the 'glossy' may recall the celebrated *glanz* fetishised by one of Freud's patients, and indeed the photographic look is ineluctably implicated in the structure of fetishism."[12]

Insofar as the photograph reveals no external marking, no touch of the hand (darkroom manipula-tions notwithstanding), that would connect the image to its material manufacture it creates the illu-sion that "the world appears to speak itself".[13] The world, of course, does not speak itself, and this is one of the ways by which the indexical subverts the iconic. In other words, that aspect of photo-graphic function that registers the trace of the real, and accordingly, material and historical reality, lies on the side of indexicality. These include actual lived social relations, as impoverished Sicilian youths undressed and modelled for a titled German photographer resident in Taormina, as well as the issue of who has access to the means of representation. To recall Marx's comment of the plight of the peasantry: "They do not represent themselves; they are represented"[14] – the Sicilian youths had no camera.

But also on the side of indexicality are those elements of the photograph that contradict or violate the protocols of painting that treat similar subjects. Instead of the wax museum perfection of, say, Alma-Tadema's or von Marées' ephebes, von Gloeden, as a photographer, necessarily worked with what he had on hand. Thus the hollow-chested, consumptive-looking youth with hair bands violates all canons of ephebic beauty; the contrast between tanned hands and faces and white bodies gives the lie to heroic nudity; the clumsy limbs of the standing boys and the black shocks of pubic hair affirm the brute materiality of the living subjects.

Significantly, it was precisely around this aspect of photographic indexicality that mid-nineteenth century debates about the propriety of the photographic nude revolved. If the nude was, by defini-tion, an aesthetic abstraction, a sublimatory ideal only adventitiously connected to the naked body, how could a photograph of an actual naked person pass muster? Unlike many other contemporary art photographers who, by various means, elided the "problem" of their models' genitals, von Gloeden appears to have revelled in them; the bigger, one might surmise, the better. (Many of his male models seem particularly well-endowed.) Given that one of the distinguishing features of the classical male nude was the diminutive size of the genitals, von Gloeden's choice of models disobeys another venerable aesthetic precept, suggesting that where it is a question of a commodity that traffics in eroticism, desire can readily trump beauty.[15]

But even if one argues that what has been lost in beauty is recuperated for desire, the critical question of whose desire nevertheless remains. Contrary to the wish-fulfilling speculations of von Gloeden's modern partisans, it is unlikely that the hundreds, if not thousands, of photographs von Gloeden and his associate Wilhelm Pluschow produced of naked boys, girls, and even children, are a function of their models' desire. On the contrary, many of the models appear bored, stupefied, or merely impassive, obediently enacting their prescribed roles and poses. While this is hardly evidence of coercion, it gives little support to the hypothesis that his models were active, much less enthusiastic participants in von Gloeden's teutonic Arcadia.[16] We should therefore reckon with another term in the photographer's deployment of beauty and desire, and that is the issue of power, less in the biographical/empirical sense of von Gloeden's wealth and privilege and his models' poverty (although this should not be minimised either), so much as in the discursive power of inscription. Thus, the power to "textualise" bodies, to make of the body of the Sicilian peasant a possessable, consumable object that provisionally confirms the photographer's, or viewers' mastery, is what links the work of von Gloeden to such photographs as that of a pair of studio-made images of two Arab men fondling each others' genitals, or, for that matter, the examples of mid-nineteenth century pornographic stereo-cartes. In the former, the staging of the models suggests an allegory of colonialism itself; the men "feminised" in terms of their posing, their identity as colonial subjects and their flaccid penises. The colonial subject is revealed as reassuringly passive and impotent; the power of inscription derives not merely from the photographer who hired and posed the models, but from a larger geo-political context. Thus, just as the encompassing terms of the patriarchal imaginary can be said to ultimately "author" the presiding conventions of heterosexual pornography and its fetishistic libidinal economy, so too is the representation of the colonial "other" a cultural product that overarches the intentions of the individual photographer.

Considered in these terms, nineteenth century illicit photographs of women or couples are as much testimonial to the workings of power as to the working of desire and the commodities it engenders. Again, it is not merely the sociological fact of working-class people who make their lives as what would now be called "sex workers" that raises the issue but, more profoundly, the ways in which the production of the imagery is effectively conjured, summoned up, incited by power:

A proliferation of sexualities through the extension of power; an optimisation of the power to which each of these sexualities gave a surface of intervention: this concatenation, particularly since the nineteenth century, has been ensured and relayed by the countless economic interests which, with the help of medicine, psychiatry, prostitution, and pornography, have tapped into both this analytic multiplication of pleasure and the optimisation of the power that controls it. Pleasure and power do not cancel or turn back against one another; they seek out, overlap, and reinforce one another. They are linked together by complex mechanisms and devices of excitation and incitement.[17]

Nowhere, however, are the processes of inscription more apparent than in the representation of the female body, and it is here that Burgin's observations on the implication of the photographic look in the structure of fetishism is most apparent. In this respect, a consideration of erotic and/or pornographic representation of has much to tell us about more mainstream representations, and the conditions and terms of their articulation. It is thus its place on a continuum of representation that makes it an instructive object for feminist analysis. As Annette Kuhn has remarked: "A deconstruction of pornography makes it possible to handle the specificity and complexity of its different forms: its cultural variability, its diverse technologies and modes of production and consumption, its status as at once commodity, industry and representation. Such an approach also insists that pornography is, after all, not that special, it is not a privileged order of representation; that it shares many of its modes of address, many of its codes and conventions, with representations which are not looked upon as a 'problem' in the way pornography is."[18]

Nineteenth century pornographic stereo-cartes and other photographic formats, unlike their deluxe daguerreotype ancestors, were hastily and of course, clandestinely manufactured and sold.[19] Where the first generation of daguerreotype pornography (c.1848–55) – especially in stereographic forms was artisanally produced, often carefully tinted or hand-coloured, the mass-produced forms were usually crudely made and relatively cheap. Their mass production was enabled by the invention of the wet plate positive/negative process, in contrast to daguerreotypes, which were unique originals. Historically speaking, such photographic imagery represents the democratisation of erotica, insofar as its lower cost and infinite reproducibility made it affordable to men of modest means and, ultimately, to working-class consumers. Where the daguerreotypes might be eligible for the category of "beauty" by virtue of their lapidary qualities, the majority of the mass-produced ones are decidedly not. Here too, desire trumps beauty, as the working-class models, who risked fines, even imprisonment for their activity, were rarely attractive, and are often ravaged and unhealthy-looking. As with the von Gloeden photographs, power is manifest in the social relations that produce the illicit subculture of the nineteenth century pornographic industry itself, with its lumpen proletariat models, and its more affluent photographic entrepreneurs, distributors and consumers.[20]

For the most part, these photographs represent what have become commonplaces of modern pornography: scenes of coitus, so-called "beaver shots" which can themselves be seen as a further corroboration of Foucault's arguments, scenes of "lesbian" sex, and, beginning in the later part of the century, homosexual scenes as well as various sadomasochist or otherwise perverse activities. The only motif that seems to have been relatively common in the nineteenth century and to have become increasingly rare in the twentieth, are images of women on chamber pots. The proliferation of "beaver shots" and the decline of those featuring simulated urination affirms the historicity of sexual practice, but so too does it affirm the persistence and durability of the deep structures of fetishistic desire. Where the imagery of idealised, beautiful and aestheticised femininity represents the disavowal of castration by transforming the feminine image into a fetish itself (a formation that Freud designated as fetishistic scopophilia), the imagery of "pornographised" femininity is characterised by a voyeuristic gaze which seeks to investigate, demystify or degrade. From whence comes the pleasure, then, of the "beaver shot" which exposes to the viewer the evidence of the woman's fantasised castration, given Freud's statement "…probably no male human being is spared the fright of castration at the sight of a female genital."?[21] In an interesting discussion of this conundrum, Paul Willeman has proposed the co-existence of another kind of look: "…porn also often plays on a second, more reassuring type of looking which can quite easily coexist with the fetishistic look, although it is in some sense its inverse. It is less a disavowal of 'her' castration than a confirmation of the viewer's phallic power. This specular relation is dependent on the emphatic direct address interpellating the viewer as possessor and donor of the phallus, the one who is required to complete the picture, as it were".[22] But, as he also points out, "In porn…it is the loss generated by the friction between the fantasy looked for and the fantasy displayed which sustains the desire for ever-promised and never-found gratification."[23] Similarly, and as Annette Kuhn remarks, "Whatever it does, pornography is, of course, exactly a commodity: it is produced and bought and sold. To the extent that porn participates in the disruptive potential of sexual passion, it is indeed dangerous merchandise. But in its attempt to articulate sexual fantasy through particular regimes of representation, pornography seeks, at the same time to contain those very qualities of fascination and disruption – in the process becoming literal, earnest, clinical. Porn is often, in consequence, profoundly disappointing to its consumers… there is always the hope, after all, that it can be assuaged by trying (and buying) again."[24]

Cindy Sherman
Untitled Film Still
1977–80

But if the pornographic representation, despite itself, risks becoming clinical, conversely, even the putatively scientific image of the female body is prone to erotic inscription, a consequence of the discursive associative train woman/sexual difference/body/eroticism. Eadweard Muybridge's representations of the female body from his *The Human Figure in Motion* provides an instructive instance. In her compelling discussion of these images, Linda Williams frames her argument with Foucault's influential formulations about the relation of power to sexuality.[25] But equally important to her argument is the hypothesis that the female body "poses a problem of sexual difference which it then becomes the work of the incipient forms of narrative and mise en scène to overcome."[26]

The Human Figure is divided into three categories: men, women and children, photographed in a gridded progression of movement from simple to more complex activity (as many as forty eight cameras were employed to register this movement). But it is specifically in the representation of the female nude that what she terms a "gratuitous fantasisation and iconisation of the women" occurs, securing, it would seem, what could be termed the "feminisation" of the female body: "Some of the movements and gestures in the women's section – walking, running, jumping – parallel those of the men. Yet even here, there is a tendency to add a superfluous detail to the women's movements – details which tend to mark her as more embedded within a socially prescribed system of objects and gestures than her male counterparts."[27]

As the sequences unfold, the women are further inscribed within a narrativised framework. For example, when the female model lies down (as does the male model), she lies down in a hammock, or in a bed; the female model is furnished with transparent wisps of fabric that accentuate her nudity; she dresses or undresses; in sequences that feature two women, they are engaged in enigmatic and subtly eroticised interactions that are altogether different from the shared activity of two men. In some of the studies one woman throws a bucket of water over another; in another, water is poured into a woman's mouth, in another, two women dance together. In another plate, the movement of the woman, hand over groin, arm shielding her face, suggests nothing so much as a woman unwillingly exposed, caught out in her vulnerable nakedness, fleeing the gaze that pursues her, a scenario that both intensifies the voyeurism of the look and underscores the sadism that may accompany voyeuristic scopophilia.

Thus, as Williams demonstrates, even when the ostensible purpose of the representation is a scientific and objective demonstration of the motor mechanisms of the body, the female body will be variously coded and inscribed in ways that signal not only its difference, but its inherent erotic significance. Moreover, this writing on the body, these processes of textualisation and narrativisation, should not be exclusively attributed to Muybridge-as-author, but should be understood as culturally authored, as well as *authorised*. Which is to say that however many factors one may integrate into a reading of an individual or collective corpus of work, one cannot dispense with an ideological critique, that is to say, an acknowledgement of the agency of culture in producing and reproducing relations of

Eadweard
Muybridge
Plate 498
Miscellaneous Phases
of the Toilet
1887

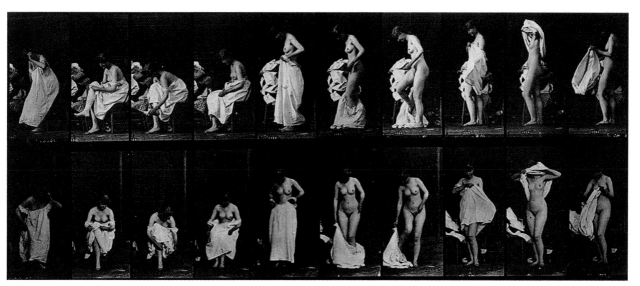

power and domination, mastery and submission. By virtue of its indexicality and its potent illusion of reality, photography, as most everyone would concur, has been an especially effective purveyor of dominant ideologies relating to gender, race and class. Moreover, and however much one wishes to grant the possibility of transformative readings, the mobility of spectatorial desire, the non-fixity of subject positions, the bisexuality of human subjectivity, and so forth, it remains the case that it is primarily within the arena of critical art practices – for example, Cindy Sherman's stunning oeuvre – that concepts of beauty and desire can be made objects of conscious and deliberate political analysis. Such practices are important not merely because they transform beauty from an attribute or quality to a problem, but because they understand desire to be no less problematic. To acknowledge the obdurate bedrock of the psyche, the unconscious, the dark continent of human subjectivity (not femininity), does not, by that token, absolve us from the political – indeed the ethical – task of decipherment, demystification and, ultimately, transformation.

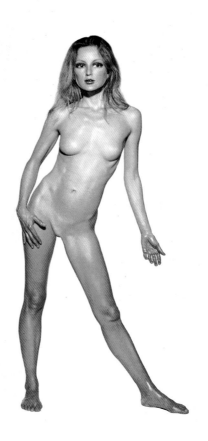

Inez van Lamsweerde
"Thank you Thighmaster", Kim
1993

1 Laura Mulvey, "Preface" in *Fetishism and Curiosity*, Indiana University Press, Bloomington and Indianapolis, 1996, p. xiv

2 André Breton, *Surrealism and Painting*, trans. Simon Watson Taylor, Harper & Row, New York, 1965, p. 1

3 Hal Foster, "Preface", in Foster (ed.), *Vision and Visuality*, Bay Press, Seattle, 1988, p. ix

4 The term is W. F. Haug's. See Haug, *Critique of Commodity Aesthetics: Appearance, Sexuality and Advertising in Capitalist Society*, University of Minnesota Press, Minneapolis, 1986

5 These are all titles of books that have appeared in the past decade; the list could, of course, be expanded

6 "When Titian arranges a purely carnal Venus, softly stretched out... in all the fullness of her perfection as goddess and as subject for paint, it is obvious that, for him, to paint meant to caress, a conjunction of two voluptuous sensations in one supreme act in which self-mastery and mastery of his medium were identified with a masterful possession of the beauty herself in every sense." Paul Valèry, "The Nude" in *The Collected Works of Paul Valèry,* Jackson Matthews (ed.), Princeton University Press, Princeton, 1956–75, v. 12, p. 48. Thanks to Shefali Srivastava for supplying this quotation

7 Francette Pacteau, *The Symptom of Beauty*, Reaktion Books, London, 1994

8 Ibid., p. 15

9 Jacqueline Rose, "Sexuality in the Field of Vision" in Rose, *Sexuality in the Field of Vision*, Verso, London, 1986, pp. 225–233

10 Contemporaries of von Gloeden who also constructed thematically similar tableaux (for example, naked boys, Greek togas, etc.) are Thomas Eakins, working in Philadelphia and F. Holland Day, working in Boston. See for example, *Eakins and the Photograph: Works by Thomas Eakins and his Circle in the Collection of the Pennsylvania Academy of the Fine Arts*, Susan Danly and the Cheryl Leibold, eds. The Smithsonian Institution Press and the Pennsylvania Academy of Fine Arts, Washington D.C. and Philedelphia,1994, and Ellen Fritz Clattenburg, *The Photographic Work of F. Holland Day*, (ex. cat.), College Museum, Wellesley, Ma., 1975

11 Victor Burgin, "Photography, Phantasy, Function" in Burgin (ed.), *Thinking Photography*, Macmillan, London, 1982, p. 189

12 Ibid., pp. 189–90. See too, in this regard, Christian Metz, "Photography and Fetish" in *October 34*, Fall 1985, pp. 81–90

13 Jean-Louis Baudry, "Effects of the Basic Cinematographic Apparatus," in Theresa Hak Kyung Cha, *Apparatus*, Tanam Press, New York, 1980, p. 28

14 Karl Marx, "The Eighteenth Brumaire of Louis Bonaparte" in Robert C. Tucker, *The Marx-Engels Reader*, W. W. Norton & Co., New York, p. 608

15 Freud did not believe that male or female genitals could be perceived as beautiful: "'Beauty' and 'attraction'," he wrote, "are originally attributes of the sexual objects. It is worth remarking that the genitals themselves, the sight of which is always exciting, are nevertheless hardly ever judged to beautiful; the quality of beauty seems instead, to attach to secondary sexual characters." Freud, *Civilization and its Discontents*, trans. James Strachey, W. W. Norton & Co., New York, 1961, p. 32. For a discussion of the reasons for the small genitals of the idealised male nude see A. Solomon-Godeau, *Male Trouble: A Crisis in Representation*, Thames & Hudson, London, 1997

16 See in this regard Peter Weiermair, "Wilhelm von Gloeden's Arcadia: Remarks on an Obsessive Oeuvre" in Tk and Gert Schiff, *Die Sonne von Taormina*, Kunstalle Basel, Basel, 1979

17 Michel Foucault, *The History of Sexuality*, trans. Robert Hurley, Pantheon Books, New York, 1978, p. 107

18 Annette Kuhn, "Lawless Seeing" in *The Power of the Image*, Routledge & Kegan Paul, London, 1985, p. 22

19 The anonymous photographs in the exhibition are from the Kinsey Institute Archive. From the circumstances under which Kinsey both collected, organised and classified what eventually became an archive of over 75,000 images is a striking confirmation of Foucault's arguments in *The History of Sexuality*. As James Crump has described this archive, "Kinsey's methodology of taxonomically ordering human sexual behaviours and their visual analogues was rooted in a lifetime of collecting that reached its apogee during his career as a scientist. The immense archive of photography should be seen in this context – of ordering, collecting, and assembling a paradigmatic visual resource that reflects usefully upon its subject, in this case human sexuality." Crump, "The Kinsey Institute Archive: A Taxonomy of Erotic Photography", *History of Photography*, vol. 18, no. 1, Spring 1994, pp. 1–12, p. 1. Compare with Foucault's description: "'Sexuality': the correlative of the slowly developed discursive practice which constitutes the *scientia sexualis*. The essential features of this sexuality are not the expression of a representation that is more or less distorted by ideology, or of a misunderstanding caused by taboos; they correspond to the functional requirements of a discourse that must produce its truth. Situated at the point of intersection of a technique of confession and a scientific discursivity, where certain major mechanisms had to be found for adapting them to one another... sexuality was defined as being "by nature": a domain susceptible to pathological processes, and hence one calling for therapeutic or normalising interventions; a field of meaning to decipher; the site of processes concealed by specific mechanisms; a focus of indefinite causal relations; and an obscure speech... that had to be ferreted out and listened to." p. 68

20 An extremely good account of the conditions and market for such photographs may be found in Elizabeth Ann McCauley *Industrial Madness: Commercial Photography in Paris 1848–1871*, Yale University Press, New Haven, 1994. For a discussion of some of the larger implications of nineteenth century erotic and pornographic photography, see my essays "Reconsidering Erotic Photography; Notes for a Project of Historical Salvage" in Solomon–Godeau, *Photography at the Dock: Essays on Photographic History, Institutions and Practices*, University of Minnesota Press, Minneapolis,1991 and "The Legs of the Countess" in *October 39*, Winter 1986, pp. 65–108

21 Sigmund Freud, "Fetishism" in *The Standard Edition of the Complete Psychological Works*, trans. and (ed.) James Strachey, Hogarth Press, London, 1951–1973, p. 155

22 Paul Willeman, "Letter to John" in *The Sexual Subject: A Screen Reader in Sexuality*, Routledge, London,1992, p. 178

23 Willeman, p. 179

24 Kuhn, p. 23

25 Linda Williams, "Film Body: An Implantation of the Perversions" in *Narrative, Apparatus, Ideology*, Philip Rosen (ed.), Columbia University Press, New York, 1986, pp. 507–534

26 Williams, p. 509

27 Williams, p. 512

Dangerous Spaces

David Elliott

"A little knowledge is a dangerous thing" my mother said to me, and no doubt countless other mothers have also given the same advice. But what did she mean? I was never really sure. Was it a warning that the water I was getting into was far too deep for my short legs? Or was it an exhortation for me to try to learn more – much more – than I could ever know?

Making a litany out of a cliché, she meant, of course, both things. But my retort was "what does a lot of knowledge look like?" A childish question perhaps, but reasonable. And one that this exhibition at least tries to take seriously. It is necessary to see the enemy and then know him better.

But are seeing and knowing the same thing? I think not. Admittedly, the word "knowledge" has a definitive ring but this is misleading. It seems finite but never actually can be so. In language it has a metaphorical "body" which may be added to. It is both a beginning and an end in itself. And if the phenomenon described as "post-modernism" should have any credibility, it has been in its qualification and revitalisation of the authority of knowledge. The Positivist, so-called modern, approach worked in straight "rational" lines according to its own internal logic. Knowledge was built progressively on other knowledge within a framework of power which, since the Enlightenment, has been defined by the nations of the western world.

Knowledge, however, has not been a commodity which anyone or everyone can attain – it could be dangerous, difficult or just too powerful – it has to be dealt with carefully, handed down, imparted, rationed.

At the heart of this is the idea that some people have knowledge and others don't. It's not such an unreasonable proposition – people's capacities, economic status and social contexts are different and the attainment of knowledge depends on all these things. But the possession of knowledge is not always necessarily related to the enjoyment of power. Under such circumstances, this may be more of a burden than a privilege; too much rather than too little knowledge can also be dangerous.

The idea of knowledge seems to imply a hierarchy in that it creates and depends on structures or patterns to which only some people have access; only recently has its authority been challenged by more "democratic" means of distribution and communication. On the postmodern network, where in theory so little can be controlled, the digested structure of knowledge is challenged by the free flow of raw information or data to which anyone may have access. Of course, a belief in this is as naive and utopian as a faith in trickle-down effects of economic progress. To even start you need the resources to buy the computer.

Thinking about the differences between facts and knowledge, we begin to realise that the hierarchies of knowledge are constructed in many different ways which have always supported each other socially and politically. The history of science is littered with such cases; the fate of Galileo is one of the best known examples. Facts are more neutral, isolated – that is, until they are put together in patterns and then they change.

Finding our way through the chaos of information – true or false – emanating from the universe, the world, its inhabitants, flora and fauna, objects and beliefs, is a daunting, if not impossible, task. Forms have to be found to give it all order; categories and types have to be created. Humanity, nature and the material world all have their specific manifestations and these have to be related to their place within the whole. It was also believed that appearances reflected essence and therefore that visual categorisation was in some sense essential. From the relatively crude visual structures – or taxonomies – which resulted from this, which confirmed (or even emerged from) "objective" documentation, an average or norm was established. Once the scale had been calibrated in this way, other things were measured through their difference.

What we see is a function of what we know, and so we begin to mould our perception of the world and the way we represent it in line with what we believe. In short, what we see is what we want to: Akira Kurosawa made this the subject of his film *Rashomon*, which told three different characters' versions of the same set of events. In the present, science – apparently unassailable and immutable because it can be measured – has become rather like a new form of religion. It is absolute and universal to some, dangerous and relative to others who don't hold the same beliefs or value the same patterns. In the unpromising and stony tundra which may be found at such extremities art, like lichen or moss, often takes hold.

The advent of photography helped intensify the aura of objectivity which was attributed to the scientific study of man and nature. The oil paintings, engravings and watercolours of Enlightenment scholarship were now replaced by what seemed to be the incontrovertible fact of the photographic image. It would have been too simple-minded, even in the 1840s, to have regarded photography as a wholly innocent new medium – its practitioners took over far too many of the genres and conventions of painting – but it gave the appearance of being an exact, unbiased replication of the real world, relatively untouched by human hand. Photographic albums of views, beauties, great men, wars, conflicts, strange cultures, art and architecture, natural phenomena, new inventions, social types, nature and cities not only documented the events, marvels and wonders of modern life but also satisfied the demand for such images. This demand grew dramatically as the means for the mass reproduction of such images became available.

But besides providing a rapidly expanding *cabinet de curiosités* for the enjoyment, delectation and instruction of the populace, photography was also put to work. Based on previous psychological treatises and visual stereotypes, the police recorded different kinds of "criminal type" as well as the scenes of violent crimes and murders. This was evidence.

Doctors fixed the physiognomy of madness, degeneracy and death and recorded for posterity the physical effects on the body of electrical and other stimuli. This was part of medicine. For anthropologists, the study of anthropometry, in which other races were photographed and measured to be compared with specimens from European cultures, was one of the building blocks of the "science" of eugenics. According to the contexts in which they appeared, Bushman, *Üntermensch* or Degenerate could also provide the visual evidence for a homily about Darwinian survival of the fittest or, most disquietingly, be enlisted as a *doppelganger* to the Aryan ideal of beauty – the nightmare opposite of *Nordische Schönheit*.[1]

In Europe during the 1930s and 1940s the unholy alliance between science and prejudice surfaced in propaganda and genocide. When the rational apparatus of the Enlightenment was enlisted by totalitarian ideologies to justify and achieve the extermination of the lives of millions,[2] the perversion of the ethical autonomy of aesthetics seemed little more than a side show.[3]

Although eugenics has long been discredited, its theories and stereotypes still remain with us. Genocide – "ethnic cleansing" – discrimination and racism are also contemporary phenomena and their panoply of images cannot be discounted. The pernicious belief that the moral and social worth (beauty) of an individual may be indicated (or even measured) in his or her physique, origin, state of health or expression is still around, although it is now more familiar in the "feelgood" worlds of fashion and advertising – in fact in any of those activities driven by fear and desire.

The battle-lines between purity and hybridity, health and degeneracy, race and identity, sexual orientation and gender, homelessness and belonging, exile and possession, belief and scepticism.
desire and frustration – all those elements which, when taken together, constitute the limits of
freedom and oppression – are fluid and strongly contested. The ill-defined, non-verbal, sometimes
dangerous, spaces which can be found between such entities are often awkward, painful. Yet they
are of essential importance for contemporary freedoms – aesthetic, intellectual, social and political
– because they hold the key to the way things are shown. With its capacity to move freely between
reality, quotation and metaphor, inventing its own patterns and structures as it continues, art,
trapped between material and spirit, sometimes ambiguous yet always finite, flourishes. It illuminates, interrogates and even – on occasion – patrols the disciplines, prejudices, ideas and phenomena which lie at the heart of this exhibition.

Manabu Yamanaka
Fujohkan [# 4]
1992

1 *Nordic Beauty*, the title of a Nazi illustrated magazine
2 Theodor Adorno and Max Horkheimer wrote *Dialectics of
   Enlightenment* in the USA towards the end of the Second World
   War, in which they regarded the rationalism of the Enlightenment
   as the origin of Fascism, because its rigidity institutionalised and
   encouraged "mythic fear". The Kantian aesthetic system, on the
   other hand, which in modified form continues to the present, created the autonomous ethical field within which modern art could
   exist. Of course within this field artists have the freedom to make
   anti – or unethical – interventions if they wish, but that does not
   alter the framework of the field. See also David Elliott,
   "Duchamp's Endgame or the fertile impossibility of 'modern art'"
   in *Heart of Darkness*, (ex. cat.), Kröller-Müller Museum, Otterlo,
   1994
3 Nazi ideas of *Entartete Kunst* (degenerate art) found their origins
   in the theories of Max Nordau, who thought that spiritual degeneracy
   expressed itself in the replication of "degenerate" or fragmented
   art forms

Exhibition Checklist

The following checklist is of the exhibition as presented in Oxford, ordered alphabetically by section.
Dimensions given are of the unframed sizes unless specified otherwise, height preceeding width.

THE MUSEUM

Roger Fenton

Greek Hero
c.1857
albumen print
35 × 24.5 cm
The Royal Photographic Society, Bath

Sculpture of Hermaphrodite
c.1855
salted paper print
38 × 27.5 cm
Michael & Jane Wilson Collection

Study of Bust of Woman
c.1850
salted paper print
33 × 23.5 cm
Michael & Jane Wilson Collection

Joan Fontcuberta

Fauna: El Guardian del Bien Total/ Der Grosse Wachter des Hochsten Wohls
Archive of Professor Peter Ameisenhaufen, c.1940
1990
6 silver gelatine prints and handwritten text
50 × 40 cm each
collection of the artist, courtesy of Helga de Alvear Gallery, Madrid

Fauna: Cercopithecus Icarocornu
Archive of Professor Peter Ameisenhaufen c.1940
1987
5 gelatine silver prints, drawing and handwritten text
50 × 40 cm each
collection of the artist, courtesy of Helga de Alvear Gallery, Madrid

Fauna: Archive of Professor Peter Ameisenhaufen c.1940
1985–1990
ephemera displayed in showcases
collection of the artist, courtesy of Helga de Alvear Gallery, Madrid

Vid Ingelevics

Axis: a tale of two stories
1995
7 black and white prints
35.6 × 27.9 cm each
courtesy of the artist

Karen Knorr

The Invention of Tradition
1988
cibachrome mounted on aluminium, in wood frame
91.5 × 89 cm
private collection, London

The Physiognomy of Taste
1990
cibachrome mounted on aluminium, in wood frame
100 × 100 cm
courtesy Maureen Paley, Interim Art

Sherrie Levine

Untitled (After Walker Evans: Negative)
1989
gelatine silver print
74 × 52.2 cm
collection Fonds Regional d'Art Contemporain des Pays de la Loire

Richard Ross

Santa Barbara Museum of Art, Santa Barbara, California
1983
c-type colour print
50.5 × 40.5 cm
courtesy the artist and L.A. Galerie, Frankfurt

Museum of Natural History, Cairo
1984
c-type colour print
50.5 × 40.5 cm
courtesy the artist and L.A. Galerie, Frankfurt

Deyrolle Taxidermy, Paris, France
1985
c-type colour print
50.5 × 40.5 cm
courtesy the artist and L.A Galerie, Frankfurt

Ashmolean Museum, Oxford, England
1985
c-type colour print
50.5 × 40.5 cm
courtesy the artist and L.A. Galerie, Frankfurt

Sir Benjamin Stone

Photographie d'une portion des Gemeaux
Observatoire de Paris
par M.M. Henry, 1887
albumen print

Photographie d'une portion de Cassiopée
(de Novembre 1886)
Observatoire de Paris
par M.M. Henry
albumen print

An Electric Spark, Positive Discharge
photo by M.A.A. Campbell Swinton, 1902
albumen print

An Electric Spark Positive Discharge
photo by M.A.A. Campbell Swinton, 1902
gelatine silver print

"Copies of early photographs taken by Mr. Fox Talbot about 1841 or 2 in an album lent me by Mr. Kenderson of Reading 1898"
B. J. Stone
platinum print

Miscellaneous album with various portraits
c.1975
albumen prints

Remains of sculptured groups surmounting the tomb of Mausolos, Greek Collection, British Museum
1907
platinum print

Copy of Fox Talbot relics in the possession of Mr. John Henderson
1898
platinum print

Sculptured Stele, Greek Collection, British Museum 1907
platinum print

Discobolus, Greek Collection, British Museum 1907
platinum print

Statue of Demeter, Greek Collection, British Museum 1907
platinum print

Miscellaneous album with various portraits including:
J. Challoner, Jockey and Battoni's Magdalena
c.1875
albumen prints
Birmingham Central Library: Sir Benjamin Stone Collection

Thomas Struth

National Gallery I, London
1989
c-type colour print in wood frame
183.5 × 199.6 cm
private collection

Hiroshi Sugimoto

The Brides in the Bath Murderer
1994
gelatine silver print
50.8 × 61 cm
courtesy Sonnabend Gallery,
New York

The Hanging
1994
gelatine silver print
50.8 × 61 cm
courtesy Sonnabend Gallery,
New York

Mass Murderer and Sexual Psychopath
1994
gelatine silver print
50.8 × 61 cm
courtesy Sonnabend Gallery,
New York

Rosamond Wolff Purcell

Uncurated miscellani: fetal pigs,
snake, moles, mice, double apple, cat's
guts, slug, frog, toad
1991
cibachrome
48.2 × 35.5 cm
Rosamond W. Purcell [Kathleen
Ewing Gallery]

Baby with closed eyes, Ruysch
specimen, Leiden
1991
cibachrome
40.5 × 47 cm
courtesy Rosamond W. Purcell

Arm holding eye socket, Collection
Albinus, Leiden
1992
cibachrome
25.4 × 15.2 cm
courtesy of Rosamond W. Purcell

ORIGINS: MYTHS & NARRATIVES

Faisal Abdu' Allah

I wanna kill uncle Sam coz he aint
my mother fuckin uncle
1994
gelatine silver print mounted
on MDF board
100 × 200 cm
courtesy of the artist

Anon

Anthropometric Studies / Academy
Figures
c.1870
5 albumen prints:
i) 29 × 22.8 cm
ii) 29 × 22.7 cm
iii) 33.5 × 25 cm
iv) 34 × 25 cm
v) 32 × 25.5 cm
courtesy of the Museum of
Mankind, British Museum,
London

New South Wales Female
c.1880
albumen print
courtesy of the Royal
Anthropological Institute of
Great Britain and Ireland

Aboriginal Female
c.1880
albumen print
courtesy of the Royal
Anthropological Institute of
Great Britain and Ireland

David A. Bailey

The Barbados / British Series
[nos. 13–18]
1989–90
6 c-type colour prints
25.4 × 30.5 cm each
courtesy of the artist

Prince Roland Bonaparte

Peaux Rouge
Album containing 35 albumen
prints
1883
various sizes
Pitt Rivers Museum, University
of Oxford, Photograph
Collection (Album 50.17ab)

Nancy Burson

Evolution II
1984
gelatine silver print
28 × 35 cm
courtesy of the artist

Mankind
1983–84
gelatine silver print
28 × 35 cm
courtesy of the artist

Charles Darwin

The Expressions of the Emotions in
Man and Animals
J. Murray, London, 1872
book
The National Museum of
Photography, Film & Television
(by courtesy of the Board of
Trustees of the Science Museum)

The Expression of the Emotions in
Man and Animals
J. Murray, London, 1873
book
courtesy of English Heritage

Carl and Frederick Dammann

Ethnographical Photographic Gallery
of the various Races of Men
Trüber, London, 1875
album containing 167 albumen
prints of various sizes
Pitt Rivers Museum, University
of Oxford Photograph Collection
(Album 60)

Duchenne de Boulogne

Le Mécanisme de la Physionomie
Humaine ou analyse electrophysiologique
de l'expression des passions
book
Vve de Jules Renouard, Paris, 1862
The National Museum of
Photography, Film & Television
(by courtesy of the Board of
Trustees of the Science Museum)

Ernst Dyche

Studio Portraits
c.1963
hand tinted gelatine silver prints
various sizes
Birmingham Central Library:
Dyche Collection

John Lamprey

Chinese Male
c.1869
albumen print
21.5 × 16.5 cm
courtesy of the Royal
Anthropological Institute of
Great Britain and Ireland

Anthropometric Study
Pole at 27, No. Poland, Glass Cutter
c.1869
albumen print
29 × 21.5 cm
courtesy of the Royal
Anthropological Institute of
Great Britain and Ireland

Dave Lewis

Haddon Photographic Collection,
Cambridge University Museum of
Anthropology and Ethnography
1995
c-type colour print
75 × 125 cm
courtesy Dave Lewis

Royal Anthropological Institute of
Great Britain and Ireland
1995
c-type colour print
75 × 125 cm
courtesy Dave Lewis

Untitled (Mapplethorpe)
1995
gelatine silver print
40 × 50 cm
courtesy Dave Lewis

Kem Lum

Mohammed And The Totems
1991
colour photograph, gloss paint,
aluminium on Forex
280 × 152 cm
courtesy Galleria Massimo de
Carlo, Milan

DISEASE & MADNESS

D.M. Bourneville &
P. Regnard

L'Iconographie Photographique de la
Salpêtrière (Service de M. Charcot)
1879–80
book
Bibliothèque Interuniversitaire
de Médecine, Paris

L'Iconographie Photographique de la
Salpêtrière (Service de M. Charcot)
1879–80
book
Royal Society of Medicine,
London

Dr. Hugh W. Diamond

Portraits of the Insane (plate 1)
1856
albumen prints mounted on
board
65.6 × 48.5 cm
Royal Society of Medicine,
London

Portraits of the Insane (plate 2)
1856
albumen prints mounted on
board
65.6 × 48.5 cm
Royal Society of Medicine,
London

Henry Hering

Puerperal Mania
c.1858
facsimile print from original
albumen photographs
25 × 20.3 cm
courtesy Bethlem Royal Hospital
Archive and Museum, London

Acute Mania
c.1858
facsimile print from original
albumen photographs
25 × 20.3 cm
courtesy Bethlem Royal Hospital
Archive and Museum, London

Convalescence after Puerperal Mania
c.1858
facsimile print from original
albumen photographs
25 × 20.3 cm
courtesy Bethlem Royal Hospital
Archive and Museum, London

Convalescence after Acute Mania
c.1858
facsimile print from original
albumen photographs
25 × 20.3 cm
courtesy Bethlem Royal Hospital
Archive and Museum, London

Ruffianism Homicide
c.1858
facsimile print from original
albumen photographs
25 × 20.3 cm
courtesy Bethlem Royal Hospital
Archive and Museum, London

Epilectic Mania-Infanticide
c.1858
facsimile print from original
albumen photographs
25 × 20.3 cm
courtesy Bethlem Royal Hospital
Archive and Museum, London

Mania Homicide
c.1858
facsimile print from original
albumen photographs
25 × 20.3 cm
courtesy Bethlem Royal Hospital
Archive and Museum, London

Acute Melancholia, Father and Son
c.1858
facsimile print from original
albumen photographs
25 × 20.3 cm
courtesy Bethlem Royal Hospital
Archive and Museum, London

Nicole Jolicoeur

Aura Hysterica
Les exercises de la passion
1992
artist's book
23 × 23 cm (folded size)
courtesy of the artist

J. Luys

Leçons cliniques sur les principaux
phenomenes de l'hypnotisme dans
leurs rapport avec la pathologie
mentale
1890
book
Bibliothèque Interuniversitaire
de Médecine, Paris

Eadweard Muybridge

Human and Animal Locomotion
Vol VIII: Abnormal Movements, Men
and Women (Nude and Semi Nude)
1872–85
collotype print
Birmingham Central Library

P. Richer, G. Tourette,
A. Londe

Nouvelle Iconographie de la
Salpêtrière fondée par J.M. Charcot
Jean-Martin
Vols. II, III, and IV
1889–91
book
Bibliothèque Interuniversitaire
de Médecine, Paris

Jo Spence & Dr. Tim
Sheard

Narratives of Dis-ease: Excised
1989
c-type colour print
63.5 × 42 cm
courtesy Terry Dennett Jo Spence
Archive

Narratives of Dis-ease: Exiled
1989
c-type colour print
63.5 × 42 cm
courtesy Terry Dennett Jo Spence
Archive

Narratives of Dis-ease: Expected
1989
c-type colour print
63.5 × 42 cm
courtesy Terry Dennett Jo Spence
Archive

Narratives of Dis-ease: Expunged
1989
c-type colour print
63.5 × 42 cm
courtesy Terry Dennett Jo Spence
Archive

Narratives of Dis-ease: Included
1989
c-type colour print
63.5 × 42 cm
courtesy Terry Dennett Jo Spence
Archive

CRIME AND DEGENERATION

Anon

Scene of crime, New York
c.1915
gelatine silver print
20.2 × 25.2 cm
New York City Department of
Records and Information Services
Municipal Archives

Scene of crime, New York
c.1915
gelatine silver print
20.2 × 25.2 cm
New York City Department of
Records and Information Services
Municipal Archives

*Park where Paul Richard 15 Lawn
Avenue was shot Christensen #529
1/17/16 file 966*
c.1915
gelatine silver print
20.2 × 25.2 cm
New York City Department of
Records and Information Services
Municipal Archives

Scene of crime, New York
c.1915
gelatine silver print
20.2 × 25.2 cm
New York City Department of
Records and Information Services
Municipal Archives

Scene of crime, New York
c.1915
gelatine silver print
25.2 × 20.2 cm
New York City Department of
Records and Information Services
Municipal Archives

Homicide
c.1915
gelatine silver print
25.2 × 20.2 cm
New York City Department of
Records and Information Services
Municipal Archives

Scene of crime, New York
c.1915
gelatine silver print
25.2 × 20.2 cm
New York City Department of
Records and Information Services
Municipal Archives

Scene of crime, New York
c.1915
gelatine silver print
25.2 × 20.2 cm
New York City Department of
Records and Information Services
Municipal Archives

Alphonse Bertillon

*Affaire de Colombes. Assassinat des
époux Mathieu
Vue de la salle à manger*
c.1900
photometric study
36 × 27 cm
Musée des Collections Historiques
de la Préfecture de Police, Paris

*Assassinat de Mme Gilles. 28, rue
Saint-Louis à Villemomble
Premiere photographie: vue du
corridor, 11 octobre 1904*
1904
photometric study
36 × 26.8 cm
Musée des Collections Historiques
de la Préfecture de Police, Paris

*Assassinat de Mme Pouillaude.
4 Janvier 1906
Affaire de la Plaine-Saint-Denis.
Vue interieure du café*
photometric study
35.8 × 26.8 cm
Musée des Collections Historiques
de la Préfecture de Police, Paris

*Fiche anthropometrique d'Alphonse
Bertillon 1912
(avec "photographie judiciaire")*
1912
imprimé + photographie
16 × 16 cm
Musée des Collections Historiques
de la Préfecture de Police, Paris

*Atelier photographique d'Alphonse
Bertillon
Séance de pose*
c.1900
photometric study
22 × 16.8 cm
Musée des Collections
Historiques de la Préfecture
de Police, Paris

*Affaire de Colombes. Assassinat des
époux Mathieu
Vue du bureau 2 janvier 1909*
1909
photographie metrique
36 × 27 cm
Musée des Collections Historiques
de la Préfecture de Police, Paris

*Assassinat de Mme Gilles, Octobre
1904
28, rue Saint-Louis à Villemomble
Seconde photographie. Photographie
stereometrique du cadavre*
1904
36 × 26.8 cm
Musée des Collections Historiques
de la Préfecture de Police, Paris

*Anthropometrie: mesuration du crane
laterale*
c.1900
22 × 17 cm
Musée des Collections Historiques
de la Préfecture de Police, Paris

Christian Boltanski

Archives
1989
artist's book

Sir Francis Galton

*Composites
Plate No I
Plate No II*
c.1882
albumen prints
45 × 56.5 cm
The Library, University College
London

Ideal Family Likenesses
Specimen of a composite
photographic portrait
1882
folio comprising albumen prints
26.3 × 20.5 cm
The Library, University College
London

*Portraits: groups I-VI respectively
illustrating a type of features common
among men convicted of crimes of
violence*
c.1882
albumen prints
26.3 × 20.5 cm
The Library, University College
London

*Six likenesses of Alexander the Great
and the composite of them in the
centre
Three composites of criminals*
c.1882
albumen prints
The Library, University College
London

*The Jewish Type
Composites
Full Face*
c.1882
albumen prints
The Library, University College
London

Circular Letter dated March 1882
1882
The Library, University College
London

August Sander

*People of the Weimar Republic / Man
of the twentieth century:
Cretin, Westerwald*
1926
silver gelatine print
21.5 × 26.5 cm
August Sander Archiv / SK
Stiftung Kultur, Cologne

Children in a home for the blind,
Duren
1930
gelatine silver print
21.5 × 26.5 cm
August Sander Archiv/SK
Stiftung Kultur, Cologne

Gipsies, Cologne
1930
gelatine silver print
21.5 × 26.5 cm
August Sander Archiv/SK
Stiftung Kultur, Cologne

Young sports pilot, Cologne
1925
gelatine silver print
21.5 × 26.5 cm
August Sander Archiv/SK
Stiftung Kultur, Cologne

Member of Adolf Hitler's SS Guard,
Cologne
1938
gelatine silver print
21.5 × 26.5 cm
August Sander Archiv/SK
Stiftung Kultur, Cologne

Confirmation candidate, Westerwald
1911
gelatine silver print
21.5 × 26.5 cm
August Sander Archiv/SK
Stiftung Kultur, Cologne

Young Nazi, Cologne
1936
gelatine silver print
21.5 × 26.5 cm
August Sander Archiv/SK
Stiftung Kultur, Cologne

The Cologne notary Dr. Quirke
1924
gelatine silver print
21.5 × 26.5 cm
August Sander Archiv/SK
Stiftung Kultur, Cologne

Revolutionaries (in the middle Erich
Muhsam), Berlin
1928
gelatine silver print
21.5 × 26.5 cm
August Sander Archiv/SK
Stiftung Kultur, Cologne

Industrialist (Arnold von Guilliame),
Cologne
1928
gelatine silver print
21.5 × 26.5 cm
August Sander Archiv/SK
Stiftung Kultur, Cologne

The Wiener Library
Collection

Germany
Compiled and arranged by Pay
Christian Carstensen, Hans
Hitzer and Friedrich Richter.
Published by the Volk und Reich
Verlag G.m.b.H. Berlin W9.
English translation: W.D. Bayles
c.1938
book
courtesy the Wiener Library,
London

Ilustrierter Beobachter, 1939, Folge 1
photograph of article on
Professor Landra visiting
concentration camps
1939
courtesy the Wiener Library,
London

Ilustrierter Beobachter, Folge 44
photograph of article on Ghetto
types, Jews
1939
courtesy the Wiener Library,
London

Two pages from [Nazi] photographic
album
1. Juden Type Lublin
2. Nochmals Polnishe Juden
c.1939
courtesy the Wiener Library,
London

SS Race Research
photograph of prisoner having
nose measured
c.1939
courtesy the Wiener Library,
London

Photograph of SS officer kneeling next
to baby in pram
c.1939
courtesy the Wiener Library,
London

MORTALITY

Gwen Akin and
Allan Ludwig

Sliced Face #2
1985
platinum/palladium print
35.5 × 28 cm
courtesy of the artists

Torso #2
1985
platinum/palladium print
82.5 × 101.6 cm
courtesy of the artists

Baby in a Bottle
1985
platinum/palladium print
82.5 × 101.6 cm
courtesy of the artists

Anon

Post mortem and memorial
photographs
1853–1905
albumen and gelatine prints
various sizes
private collection

Murder victims: England, Scotland,
Wales. The Daily Herald Archive
1935–62
11 photographs
various sizes
National Museum of Photography,
Film & Television (by courtesy of
the Board of Trustees of the
Science Museum)

Andres Serrano

The Morgue (Infectious Pneumonia)
1992
cibachrome, silicone, plexi-glass,
wood frame
96 × 114.8 cm
collection of the artist

The Morgue (Death by Drowning II)
1992
cibachrome, silicone, plexi-glass,
wood frame
96 × 114.8 cm
courtesy Paula Cooper Gallery,
New York

The Morgue (Burnt to Death)
1992
cibachrome, silicone, plexi-glass,
wood frame
96 × 114.8 cm
courtesy Paula Cooper Gallery,
New York

Wilhelm von Roentgen

The bones of a hand with a ring on
one finger, viewed through X-ray
1895
photoprint from radiograph
(facsimile copy)
24.1 × 17.6 cm
courtesy of The Wellcome Trust,
London

Manabu Yamanaka

Fujohkan [# 4]
1992
gelatine silver print
110.5 × 193.8 cm
courtesy of the artist

THE CULTURE OF NATURE

Karl Blossfeldt

Cajaphova lateritia
*c.*1926
gelatine silver print (reprint)
40 × 30 cm
Karl Blossfeldt Archive, Ann and Jürgen Wilde, Cologne

Cucurbita
tendrils of a pumpkin, magnified four times
*c.*1926
gelatine silver print (reprint)
40 × 30 cm
Karl Blossfeldt Archive, Ann and Jürgen Wilde, Cologne

Papaver orientalis
*c.*1926
gelatine silver print (reprint)
40 × 30 cm
Karl Blossfeldt Archive, Ann and Jürgen Wilde, Cologne

Delphinium-Larkspur
part of a dried leaf magnified six times
*c.*1926
gelatine silver print (reprint)
40 × 30 cm
Karl Blossfeldt Archive, Ann and Jürgen Wilde, Cologne

Dipsacus Laciniatus
Teasel, leaves dried on the stem magnified four times
*c.*1926
gelatine silver print (reprint)
40 × 30 cm
Karl Blossfeldt Archive, Ann and Jürgen Wilde, Cologne

Impatiens Glandulifera
Indian Balsam, stem with branches, life-sized
*c.*1926
gelatine silver print (reprint)
40 × 30 cm
Karl Blossfeldt Archive, Ann and Jürgen Wilde, Cologne

Chris Bucklow

Host: Dianthus Chris Eubank (Dianthus caesium X D.Whaithman's Beauty)
1990
c-type colour prints mounted on wood
21 × 30.5 × 4 cm each
courtesy Laurent Delaye Gallery, London

Host (Pyrus communis-Cratageous oxyacantha / Pear hawthorn tree)
1990
c-type colour prints mounted on wood
21 × 30.5 × 4 cm each
courtesy Laurent Delaye Gallery, London

Cor Dera

Hummingbirds (series 18)
1993
collage
28.5 × 30.3 × 1.2 cm (each part)
courtesy Torch Gallery, Amsterdam

Untitled (series 20)
1993
collage
8.5 × 8 × 1.2 (each part)
courtesy Torch Gallery, Amsterdam

Seabirds of the world (series 16)
1993
collage
5.2 × 6 × 1.2 (each part)
courtesy Torch Gallery, Amsterdam

Joan Fontcuberta

Herbarium
Cardus fibladissus
1985
gelatine silver bromide, selerium tone
26 × 22 cm
collection of the artist, courtesy of Helga de Alvear Gallery, Madrid

Herbarium
Karchofa sardinae
1983
gelatine silver bromide, selerium tone
26 × 22 cm
collection of the artist, courtesy of Helga de Alvear Gallery, Madrid

Herbarium
Guillumeta polymorpha
1982
gelatine silver bromide, selerium tone
26 × 22 cm
collection of the artist, courtesy of Helga de Alvear Gallery, Madrid

Herbarium
Philocactus chumba
1984
gelatine silver bromide, selerium tone
26 × 22 cm
collection of the artist, courtesy of Helga de Alvear Gallery, Madrid

Herbarium
Rasputina eclectica
1982
gelatine silver bromide, selerium tone
26 × 22 cm
collection of the artist, courtesy of Helga de Alvear Gallery, Madrid

Herbarium
Fungus Mungus
1982
gelatine silver bromide, selerium tone
26 × 22 cm
collection of the artist, courtesy of Helga de Alvear Gallery, Madrid

Edward Fox

The Anatomy of Foliage, no. 8
Spanish Chestnut, Buxted Park, Sussex
1864–1865
2 albumen prints
29 × 22 cm each
private collection

The Anatomy of Foliage, no. 1
Sycamore, Preston, near Brighton
1864–1865
2 albumen prints
29 × 22 cm each
private collection

Eadweard Muybridge

Human and Animal Locomotion
Volume XI: Wild Animals and Birds
1872–85
collotype prints
Birmingham Central Library

Human and Animal Locomotion
Volume X Domestic Animals
1872–82
collotype prints
Birmingham Central Library

Hiroshi Sugimoto

Day Seascapes: English Channel
1994
gelatine silver print
50.8 × 60 cm
courtesy Sonnabend Gallery, New York

Day Seascapes: Aegean Sea, Pilion
1990
gelatine silver print
50.8 × 60 cm
courtesy Sonnabend Gallery, New York

Day Seascapes: Ligurian Sea, Saviore
1993
gelatine silver print
50.8 × 60 cm
courtesy Sonnabend Gallery, New York

Day Seascapes: Marmar Sea, Silivli
1991
gelatine silver print
50.8 × 60 cm
courtesy Sonnabend Gallery,
New York

THE EVERYDAY

Anon

Polyfoto
c.1957
2 × 20 sheets – Ilford sportsman
camera 35mm
30 × 22.5 cm
National Museum of
Photography, Film & Television
(Board of Trustees of the Science
Museum)

Polyfoto
1960
48 sheets – Ilford sportsman
camera 35mm
30 × 22.5 cm
National Museum of
Photography, Film & Television
(Board of Trustees of the Science
Museum)

Diane Arbus

Four People at a Gallery Opening,
N.Y.
1968
gelatine silver print
50.8 × 40.6 cm
Estate of Diane Arbus, courtesy
Robert Miller Gallery, New York

Untitled (3)
1970–71
gelatine silver print
50.8 × 40.6 cm
Estate of Diane Arbus, courtesy
Robert Miller Gallery, New York

Lady in a Rooming House Parlour,
Albion, N.Y.
1963
gelatine silver print
50.8 × 40.6 cm
Estate of Diane Arbus, courtesy
Robert Miller Gallery, New York

Eugene Atget

Boutique Louis XVI Quai Bourbon
No. 8926
c.1900
albumen silver print
22 × 18 cm
Michael & Jane Wilson Collection

Hôtel du President Mascarani
No.4224
c.1900
albumen silver print
22 × 18 cm
Michael & Jane Wilson Collection

Hôtel de Lauzin No. 4969
c.1900
albumen silver print
22 × 18 cm
Michael & Jane Wilson Collection

Au Tambour 63 Quai de la Tournelle
c.1900
albumen silver print
22 × 18 cm
Michael & Jane Wilson Collection

Hôtel d'Ambrum, Quai de Bethune
No.3791
c.1900
albumen silver print
22 × 18 cm
Michael & Jane Wilson Collection

Maison D'Anne de Pisseleu No. 6677
c.1900
albumen silver print
22 × 18 cm
Michael & Jane Wilson Collection

Bernd & Hilla Becher

Framework Houses-Wiesenstrasse 35,
Siegen
1970
12 duotone offset prints
82 × 76.5 cm each
courtesy Sonnabend Gallery,
New York / Sundell Editions

Boris Becker

Bunker Series
(Group 1)
1986–88
12 gelatine silver prints
courtesy of the artist, Galerie
Ulrich Fiedler, Cologne

Bunker Series
(Group 2)
1986–88
12 gelatine silver prints
courtesy of the artist, Galerie
Ulrich Fiedler, Cologne

Ernest Dyche

Studio Portraits
c.1953
gelatine silver prints
various sizes
Birmingham Central Library:
Dyche Collection

Dan Graham

Diner on Highway, Staten Island, N.Y.
View from Window of Highway from
Restaurant, Jersey City, N.J.
1967; 1969
c-prints
27.6 × 34 cm; 22.3 × 34 cm
courtesy Marian Goodman
Gallery, New York

Highway Restaurant, Seattle
Bedroom Suite, "Model House", Staten
Island, N.Y.
1974; 1967
c-prints
27.3 × 34.4 cm, 24 × 34.8 cm
courtesy Marian Goodman
Gallery, New York

Sol LeWitt

Autobiography
1980
artist's book
courtesy of Sol LeWitt

Ed Ruscha

Twentysix Gasoline Stations
1962
artist's book
25.4 × 20.2 cm
courtesy of Ed Ruscha

Thirtyfour Parking Lots
1967
artist's book
25.4 × 20.2 cm
courtesy of Ed Ruscha

Humphrey Spender

Mass Observation
1937–38
8 photographs
various sizes
Bolton Museum & Art Gallery

Arne Svenson

Faggots [# 6, 11, 27, 30, 33, 42]
1994
gelatine silver print
50.5 × 40.3 cm
courtesy of Arne Svenson

Gillian Wearing

Signs that say what you want them
to say and not signs that say what
someone else wants you to say
1992–93
8 c-type photographic prints
mounted on aluminium
42 × 30 cm
courtesy Maureen Paley, Interim
Art

BEAUTY & DESIRE

Ajamu

C. J.
1993
gelatine silver print
71 × 51.4 cm
courtesy of Ajamu

Self Portrait
1993
gelatine silver print
36.2 × 33 cm
courtesy of Ajamu

Anon

From the category: *Humour*
gelatine silver print
The Kinsey Institute for Research
in Sex, Gender and Reproduction,
Indiana University
c.1925

From the category: *Transvestite*
c.1959
gelatine silver print
The Kinsey Institute for Research
in Sex, Gender and Reproduction,
Indiana University

From the category: *Physical
Culture*
before 1949
gelatine silver print
The Kinsey Institute for Research
in Sex, Gender and Reproduction,
Indiana University

From the category: *Sadomasochism*
1940–45
gelatine silver print
the Kinsey Institute for Research
in Sex, Gender and Reproduction,
Indiana University

From the category: *Catalogue*
1880–90
gelatine silver print
The Kinsey Institute for Research
in Sex, Gender and Reproduction,
Indiana University

From the category: *Heterosexual*
1903
gelatine silver print
The Kinsey Institute for Research
in Sex, Gender and Reproduction,
Indiana University

From the category: *Fetish. Corset*
1942
gelatine silver print
The Kinsey Institute for Research
in Sex, Gender and Reproduction,
Indiana University

From the category: *Anthropology,
Japan*
1948
gelatine silver print
The Kinsey Institute for Research
in Sex, Gender and Reproduction,
Indiana University

E.J. Bellocq

Untitled (Storyville Portraits)
c.1912
reprinted by Lee Friedlander
8 photographs, printing-out
paper, gold-toned
4 25.4 × 20.3 cm
4 20.3 × 25.4 cm
courtesy Fraenkel Gallery,
San Francisco

Philip Benson

Marilyn Monroe
1997
12 computer generated
photographs
35.5 × 21 cm each
courtesy Philip Benson

Vincenzo Galdi

Untitled (Nude with fishing net)
c.1890
albumen print
22.3 × 16 cm
private collection

Untitled (Nude Boy on a Wall)
c.1890
albumen print
22.5x 16. cm
private collection

Joy Gregory

Objects of Beauty; Shoes
1995
callotype on watercolour paper
57 × 67 cm
courtesy of the artist

Objects of Beauty; Corset
1995
callotype on watercolour paper
57 × 67 cm
courtesy of the artist

Objects of Beauty; Eyelash Curlers
1995
callotype on watercolour paper
57 × 67 cm
courtesy of the artist

Objects of Beauty; Comb
1995
callotype on watercolour paper
57 × 67 cm
courtesy of the artist

G. Pluschow

*Untitled (Girl in Beaded Skirt with
Tambourine)*
c.1890
albumen print
22.8 × 16.4 cm
private collection

*Untitled (Nude Boy and Girl Near a
Wall)*
c.1890
albumen print
22.5 × 16 cm
private collection

Eadweard Muybridge

*Plate 498 Miscellaneous Phases of the
Toilet*
1887
collotype
Michael & Jane Wilson Collection

*Human and Animal Locomotion
Volume VII: Men and Women (Nude)*
1872–85
collotype print in book
Birmingham Central Library

Cindy Sherman

*Untitled Film Still (# 3, 13, 18, 27,
37, 44)*
1977–80
photographs
40.6 × 50.8 cm each
Saatchi Collection, London

Inez van Lamsweerde

"Thank you Thighmaster", Kim
1993
c-print, perspex, dibond
185 × 120 cm
courtesy Torch Gallery,
Amsterdam

Baron Wilhelm von Gloedon

Untitled study of three young boys
c.1900
albumen print
24 × 17 cm
private collection

Untitled Boy with Flute
c.1900
platinum print
39 × 28 cm
private collection

Untitled Boy Wearing Black Lace
c.1900
albumen print
22 × 16 cm
private collection

Selected Bibliography

Armstrong, C., "Biology, Destiny, Photography: Difference According to Diane Arbus", *October 66*, Fall 1993

Barthes, R., *Camera Lucida: Reflections on Photography*, Hill & Wang, 1981

Benjamin, W., "The Work of Art in the Age of Mechanical Reproduction", *Illuminations,* Schocken Books, 1969

Beyond Ars Medica: Treasures from the Mütter Museum (ex. cat.), Thread Waxing Space, 1995

Black, J. *The Aesthetics of Murder: A Study in Romantic Literature and Contemporary Culture*, John Hopkins University Press, 1991

Bronson, A.A. and P. Gale (eds.), *Museums by Artists*, Toronto, 1983

Burrows, A. and I. Schumacher, *Portraits of the Insane: The Case of Dr. Diamond*, Quartet Books, 1990

Cartwright, L., *Screening the Body: Tracing Medicine's Visual Culture*, University of Minnesota Press, 1995

Clarke, G. (ed.), *The Portrait in Photography*, Reaktion Press, 1992.

Clifford, J., "On Ethnographic Surrealism", *The Predicament of Culture*, Harvard University Press, 1988

Cooke, L. and P. Wollen (eds.), *Visual Display – Culture Beyond Appearances*, Bay Press Seattle, 1995

Crimp, D., *On the Museum's Ruins*, MIT Press, 1993

Crump, J., "The Kinsey Institute Archive: A Taxonomy of Erotic Photography", *History of Photography*, vol. 18, no. 1, Spring 1994

Daston, L. and P. Galiston, "The Image of Objectivity", *Representations,* no. 40, Fall 1992

Dennis, K., "Ethno-Pornography: Veiling the Dark Continent", *History of Photography*, vol. 18, no. 1, Spring 1994

Durden, M. and R. Roberts (eds.), *Photography Reviewed 1968–1997*, John Hansard Gallery, University of Southampton (forthcoming 1997)

Durden, M. "Fictions and History: The Books of Christian Boltanski", *act No. 1 – Writing Art*, ed. Juliet Steyne, Pluto Press, 1995

Edwards, E., "Photographic types: The Pursuit of Method", Visual Anthropology, No. 3 (2–3), 1990; Edwards, E. (ed.), *Anthropology and Photography 1860-1920*, Yale University Press

Elliott, D., "Introduction", *Karl Blossfeldt Photographs*, Museum of Modern Art Oxfrord, 1978

Elsner, J., and R. Cardinal (eds.), *The Cultures of Collecting*, Reakton Books, 1994

Foucault, M., *The Order of Things: An Archeology of the Human Sciences*, Vintage Books, 1975

Fox, D.M. and C. Lawrence, *Photographing Medicine: Images and Power in Britain and America since 1840*, Greenwood Press, 1988

Gilman, S., *Seeing the Insane*, J. Wiley & Sons, 1982

Gilman, S., *The Face of Madness: Hugh W. Diamond and the Origin of Psychiatric Photography*, Brunner-Mazel, 1976

Gould, S.J., *The Mismeasure of Man*, W.W. Norton & Co., 1981

Green, D., "Veins of Resemblance: Photography and Eugenics", *Oxford Art Journal*, 7.2, 1984

Green, D., "Classified Subjects – Photography and Anthropology: the Technology of Power", *Ten.8*, no. 14, 1984

Greenberg, R., B.W. Ferguson and S. Nairne (eds.), *Thinking About Exhibitions*, Routledge, 1996

Greenblatt, S., "Resonance and Wonder" in Karp, I. and S.D. Lavine (eds.), *Exhibiting Cultures: The Poetics and Politics of Museum Display*, Smithsonian Institution Press, 1991

Hall, S., "Reconstruction Work", in Holland, P. and J. Spence, eds. *Family Snaps: The Meanings of Domestic Photography*, Virago, 1991

Harrison, T. and C. Madge, *Britain by Mass-Observation* (originally published in 1939), Cresset Library edition with photographs by Humphrey Spender and introduction by Angus Calder, 1986

Hooper-Greenhill, E., *Museums and the Shaping of Knowledge*, Routledge, 1992.

Jay, M., "Scopic Regimes of Modernity", in H. Foster (ed.), *Vision and Visuality*, Bay Press Seattle, 1988

Krauss, R., *Cindy Sherman 1975–1993*, Rizzoli, 1993

Lalvani, S., *Photography, Vision and the Production of Modern Bodies*, SUNY Press, 1996

Lesser, W., *Pictures at an Execution: An Inquiry Into the Subject of Murder*, Harvard University Press, 1995

MacClancy, J., "Brief Encounter: the Meeting, in Mass-observation, of British Surrealism and Popular Anthropology", *Journal of the Royal Anthropological Institute*, September 1995, vol. no. 3

Malcolm, J., "The Real Thing" (Review of "Bellocq: Photographs from Storyville, the Red-Light District of New Orleans", Random House, 1996), *The New York Review*, January 1997

Malraux, A., "Museum Without Walls", *The Voices of Silence*, Doubleday & Co, 1953

Marable, D., "Photography and Human Behaviour in the Nineteenth Century", *History of Photography*, vol. 9, no. 2, 1985

Mercer, K., "The Camera as Kinky Machine: Notes on Ajamu's Photographs", *Black Bodyscapes*, edited and published by David A. Bailey, 1994

Mercer, K., *Welcome to the Jungle: New Positions in Black Cultural Studies*, Routledge, 1994

Mulford, J., *Worktown People: Photographs from Northern England 1937–38 by Humphrey Spender*, Falling Wall Press, 1982

Nesbit, M., *Atget's Seven Albums*, Yale University Press, 1992

Pacteau, F., *The Symptom of Beauty*, Reaktion Books, 1994

Pick, D., *Faces of Degeneration: A European Disorder c.1848 c.1918*, Cambridge University Press, 1989

Ruby, J., *Secure the Shadow: Death and Photography in America*, MIT Press, 1995

Sante, L., *Evidence*, Noonday Press, 1992

Segal, L., and M. McIntosh, *Sex Exposed: Sexuality and the Pornography Debate*, Virago, 1992

Sekula, A., "The Body and the Archive", *October* 39: 1986, pp. 1–64

Sekula, A., "The Traffic in Photographs", 1981, in *Photography Against the Grain: Essays and Photo Works 1973-1983*, NSCAD Press, 1984, pp. 77–101

Showalter, E., *The Female Malady: Women, Madness and English Culture 1830-1980*, Virago, 1981.

Solomon-Godeau, A., *Photography at the Dock: Essays on Photographic History, Institutions, and Practices*, University of Minnesota Press, 1991

Spence, J., *Putting Myself in the Picture*, Camden Press, 1986

Spence, J., *Cultural Sniping: The Art of Transgression*, Routledge, 1995

Stafford, B.M., *Good Looking: Essays on the Virtue of Images*, MIT Press, 1996

Stewart, S., *On Longing: Narratives of the Miniature, the Giganic, the Souvenir, the Collection*, Duke University Press, 1993

Tagg, J., *The Burden of Representation: Essays on Photographies and Histories*, Macmillan, 1988

The Impossible Science of Being: Dialogues Between Anthropology and Photography (ex. cat.), The Photographers Gallery, 1995

Williams, L., "Film Body: An Implantation of Perversions" in *Narrative Apparatus, Ideology*, (ed.) Philip Rosen, Columbia University Press, 1996

Williams, L., "Corporealized Observers: Visual Pornographies and the 'Carnal Density of Vision'", (ed.) Patrice Petro, *Fugitive Images: From Photography to Video*, India University Press, 1995

Williams, V. and G. Hobson, *The Dead* (ex. cat.), National Museum of Photography, Film and Television, Bradford, 1996

Published by the Museum of Modern Art Oxford
30 Pembroke Street, Oxford OX1 1BP
on the occasion of the touring exhibition:

In Visible Light:
Photography and Classification in Art, Science and The Everyday
16 March – 6 July 1997

Curated by Russell Roberts

Edited by Chrissie Iles and Russell Roberts

Exhibition organised and catalogue co-ordinated by Astrid Bowron,
assisted by Elena Fernandez and Clare Manchester.
Tour organised by Rebecca Coates

The exhibition has been supported by Oxford University Press
Catalogue supported by the Elephant Trust

Designed by Herman Lelie
Production coordinated by Uwe Kraus GmbH
Printed in Italy

Additional photography by Christopher Moore and Heini Schneebeli

ISBN 0 905 836 96 0
A catalogue record of this publication is available from the British Library

Front cover: *Scene of crime, New York*, from the New York City Department of Records and Information Services Municipal Archives *c.*1915
Back cover: Karl Blossfeldt, *Dipsacus Laciniatus Teasel, leaves dried on the stem magnified four times c.*1926